"A nod to the lives of many Canadian families. This story opens ... floodgates for memories, emotions, and childhood nostalgia. These are the tales that need to be told."

Blythe George
Pickering Book Club

"This book flows like the Pefferlaw River. I couldn't put it down. *No Poverty Between the Sheets* is a romp through Pauline's childhood years, enhanced by the spicy language of her mixed French Canadian and Irish heritage. A horse theme weaves its way throughout this book and eventually has everything to do with the ending. You'll laugh out loud, and also cry. The book is a testament to her father, John Kiely, and his unfaltering love of his family."

Rod Urquhart, Editor of
Voice of the Farmer
Horse Talk Magazine

"*No Poverty Between the Sheets* made me laugh and cry. It took me back to places I have lived and I feel like I've known this author all my life!"
Cheryl Ann Spears

"Cozy, warm, funny, and a truly relatable book. Takes us back to a time when being politically correct was not the norm: just people living life."
Christine Gonsalves,
Pickering Book Club

No Poverty between the Sheets

A Memoir

by Pauline Kiely

Pauline Kiely
598 Elm Tree Rd,
Little Britain, Ontario CANADA K0M 2C0

e-book available on Amazon.com

Cover Photo: *Yolande Beaulieu – 1946*
Pilot's Licence *courtesy of Ross Tripp*
Photo of Laurel & Hardy *courtesy of Mick Kiely*
Logo *by Greg Allen*
Author Photo *courtesy of Michael Bryant*
Dave Devall photo *by Lindsey MacDonald*

Published by A Passionate Pen
Email: apassionatepen@gmail.com
Telephone: 289 512-8721

Printed by HALL'S PRINTING, 59 Durham St. W., Lindsay ON K9V 2P7
Printed in Canada

ISBN 978-1-927396-00-1

6   7   8   9   10

For my children

their children,

and their children's children.

Eternally grateful to Joan Fahey

Thanks also to Susan Reynolds

John Kiely at Dun Laoghaire pier - 1964

"We're all links in the chain of life, and this I believe is life everlasting."

—*John Francis Kiely*

Yolande Kiely and family - 2010

"Your children become the jewels in your crown."

—*Yolande Lucille Marie Kiely*

nee Beaulieu

Table of Contents

Chapter One

The Push that was the Shove

I was born under a Gemini sun and a Gemini moon, in the sixth month, on the twelfth day, in 1961. A year that spins around. Apparently the event took place with no complications about eight fifteen on that sunny June morning in Toronto East General Hospital. Other than Doctor Taylor being a 'looker', my Mother doesn't remember much because in those days a woman was practically knocked out, and when she came to she'd had a baby. Nothing out of the ordinary, simply the product of egg meets sperm and nine month's incubation. I imagine I was washed, weighed, measured, and pricked before being introduced to my Mom.

My Father was on a construction site when I arrived. His wife had been awake most of the night before, running back and forth to the toilet. She nudged him around six to drive her to the hospital. She said she had a pan of cornstarch by their bed because at the end of the pregnancy her feet would get very itchy during the night. She smiles at the memory of trails of her white footprints.

She said that when they arrived at the hospital, he signed her in, gave her the usual two kisses good-bye, and went off to bang nails. But he was sent home at ten o'clock because on break he says to *Louie the Wop*, "My wife's in the hospital having a baby."

Louie laughed at him and said, "Don't you think you should be there?"

Then my Father said, "If I need any shit from you, I'll squeeze your head. That stuff is women's work. They make the babies and bread, and we bring home the bacon."

Then the man in charge wearing the white hard-hat sent him home.

My Father gave it to you straight. He told it like it was. He said he was "the man of steel", and could prove it too 'cause on occasion he had rust in his underwear. John Francis Kiely with his sister, Mary Theresa, touched down in Toronto from Dublin on May 18, 1958. He was seventeen, and she had just turned twenty-one. The Kielys hailed from the seafront village of Dalkey, located eight miles south of the *Fair City*.

My Mother was raised in the tiny village of Alban. She calls her hometown, "a piss hole in a snow bank". Alban, just north of the French River in Northern Ontario, is an old logging town. It is a speck on a map of the Canadian Shield.

He was the fourth of ten children, and she the baby of twelve. He had grade eight, and she had grade seven. When I came along he was twenty, and she was nineteen. He spoke Irish brogue, and French was her first language. He grew up poor, and she grew up poorer.

He told me that I was made in the dark, and in a hurry, in the backseat of a '53 Buick Hudson Jet. He said he had asked my Mother for a dance about a year and a half before at the Masonic Lodge just north of Bloor on Yonge Street; and they were planning on getting married. They just weren't planning on me attending the wedding.

He said, "You were the push that was the shove."

Being Catholic, he sought advice in confession, "Father, I've made a girl pregnant."

"Do you love her?" the priest asked.

"I think I do, Father."

"If you dip your wick, you have to pay for the oil, Son." So that was that.

My Dad claimed he was a thoroughbred: a man with a horse's appetite who has pure Irish-blood. He was an inch and a pinch shy of six feet, and supported by big bones in tight skin. At twenty-one he had black hair and grey blue eyes. He was a carpenter and smelled like cut timber. He called his big hands shovels. They were calloused, and he used a magnifying glass to see the slivers that he pulled from them.

My Mother was a fine French-Canadian filly, Yolande Lucille Marie Beaulieu. My Father said, "She was a hot little number whose ass did a jig of its own when she walked." Mom is five one and a half inches tall, and she insists that is tall where she comes from. She had an hour-glass figure, thick chestnut hair, and chocolate eyes. He said she was irresistible. My Mom left home at fifteen and came to Toronto to work and to share a Munroe Street apartment with her sister, Anne.

The Beaulieu's were raised among black bear and blueberries. Her memories of home in Alban included a three-bedroom tar-paper shack. It had an outdoor outhouse, and a woodstove. They slept six to a bed and sometimes there were more living things in her bed, like lice and bed bugs.

My Mother says, "My sister Anne had spent a summer helping an aunt on their dairy farm. This aunt might have had a new baby. I don't know why Anne was sent there. All I know is that this aunt had a large family, that they did a lot of cooking, and that when my sister returned she was plump, and a good cook.

My Mother has no memory of her father, Eugene Beaulieu. He passed away on May 7, 1941, and she came into the world on December 22nd of that year.

Aunt Bette said, "Dad was a simple farmer who'd had an operation in Sudbury on his goitre, but didn't have the time or money to take the train for the thirty-mile journey to buy his medication."

Uncle Gill said, "I thought he was sleeping under an apple tree on *The Farm*."

The older children in the family remember the good days with their father. He was said to have been a big, very proud, and pious man.

Auntie Agnes told me that on every New Year's Day tears streamed down her father's face as his family prayed the Rosary, and that he would bless them individually for the New Year. She said, "He thanked God for each of us, his sons and his daughters: Gilbert, Lea, Oscar, Bette, Paul, Agnes, George, Dolores, John, Anne, Gabriel. But he wasn't there to bless the new baby, Yolande, who arrived just in time for Christmas on the shortest day of the year."

The Beaulieu family with a neighbour (top left)

Mom said, "There was loose talk in Alban, questioning the parish priest as to whether I should be baptised. After all, my Mother had been in the barn, with men, after her husband's death. My Mother was selling their life, their farm, the livestock, and machinery. I'd be hard pressed to believe that the first thoughts of a mourning widow with eleven mouths to feed would be a roll in the hay with her neighbour's husband, or a relative."

The Second World War was going on. Food was rationed. There was no pension or income for this widow back in 1941. The Parish played an important role in these small communities, keeping records of births, weddings, deaths.

The village priest showed compassion for my grandmother more than once. Her eldest daughter, Lea, married Ernest Marchand on the May 21st, 1946, and moved to the mining town of Val d'or in Quebec. She had a weak heart, but died May 18, 1953, from a lung infection. Lea left behind four daughters under the age of six: Alice, Celine, Jacqueline, and Yvette.

Jack, John, Yolande Kiely, Alice and Paul Beaulieu - 1960

My Mother says, "Father Campeau lent us his truck, and your Uncle Gill made a plywood box for the back of it. The gang of us all piled in, and Gill drove. My Mother and Johnny Dionne, Bette's husband, rode in the cab. It was dark and cold, and a long night on rough dirt roads, if you call cow paths roads. We were all huddled together to stay warm. When Gill got tired,

Johnny drove. My Mother was very grateful we made it at all. Not long after Lea's funeral, Ernest showed up in Alban with the girls."

My Mother said she was nervous about visiting her family in the family way. Apparently her mother was not thrilled by their news, and didn't understand this generation that put the cart before the horse. Her comment, "Every piss pot needs a lid." And my uncles set the bounty at a case of beer for my Mother's hand.

On November 26, 1960, my parents, the 'holy smoke combination,' were joined in holy matrimony at Holy Name Catholic Church in Toronto on Danforth Avenue. Her sister Anne served as her maid-of-honour, and Jerry Sharkey was my Father's right arm. My Mother says she put all her brothers' names in a hat, and drew Paul's name; so he walked her down the aisle. She said that her teeth chattered when she repeated her vows. Pictures show an exaggerated grin on my Father.

Apparently the day was remarkably mild and they posed for a few snaps on the steps of the church. Her dress had sequins and pearls, and plenty of lace over a crinoline hoop. Their matching bands were plain white and yellow gold. Tissue bows and paper streamers camouflaged the rusty spots on the Buick where, locked in the trunk, was a case of twelve Red Cap ale for her thirsty brothers.

During the meal teaspoons bounced off wine glasses, a custom that demands a kiss from the bride and groom. Sixty odd members from her side were in attendance. Standing for him were Sharkey, his sister Theresa, his Father, Jack, with his mistress Caroline, and their son.

Theresa remembers, "John and I had barely digested the ham sandwiches we'd eaten in a lounge at Montreal Airport, the sandwiches Mammy had made us for the journey. Then, wow, we were introduced to my Father's friend, and our half-brother Seamus upon arrival at Malton Airport in Toronto. Canada in all its glory had come at a high price."

John and Yolande Kiely on their wedding day - 1960

My Father was not impressed, and had little or no patience for the loud redhead his Da was sporting. Years later when we looked at their wedding photos, I made the mistake of asking, "Who is that?"

His answer, "Caroline. She was the image of a harvest frog in that dress. Fat through the middle, with bulging eyes, and a long sticky tongue waiting to snap up the change that fell from my old man's pockets."

As newlyweds, Mom said they played house. "One payday John bought a reel-to-reel tape recorder. He would put the microphone on my belly and record your heart beating."

Thankfully, my Mother threw out her prescription for Thalidomide. She told her doctor, "My Mother never had these drugs." Mom said, "I wasn't really sure how you were going to come out, but I knew babies were born every day."

I was a healthy seven pounds, four ounces, twenty-one inches long, strong, with a mass of dark hair. My Father wanted to name me Polly-Anna because he'd so enjoyed the film starring Hailey Mills. Mom put her little foot down, and they settled on Pauline Ann.

My Mother says, "It was the stupidest thing. A ward of new mothers in sterilized sheets and gowns, feeding newborn babies sterilized bottles of sterilized formula, while puffing away on cigarettes." She was glad to see my Father. He said he never minded that I was a girl, especially after I was chosen by the nurses for their bathing-a-newborn demonstration.

Two weeks later I was christened; and afterwards, there was a light lunch in their basement apartment. My grandfather, Jack Kiely, with white hair and thick bi-focal glasses had aged beyond his years. He offered his son a drop of whiskey the day I was baptised, and my Father's virgin throat swallowed the liquid gold. He wouldn't be twenty-one until September.

When I was about two, my fleur-de-lis Mother, shamrock Father, and their maple leaf daughter moved into a little white house in Markham, a rental from his boss, Michael Wade.

Dad called me Molly Mouse, and this was his idea of a lullaby;

> *"Molly Mouse was a hat-check girl, woo hoo!*
> *Molly Mouse was a hat-check girl,*
> *He thought he'd give that chick a whirl,*
> *ah ha, ah ha, woo hoo!*
> *Oh, Molly Mouse, won't you marry me, ah ha,*
> *Molly Mouse, won't you marry me, woo hoo?*
> *Not without uncle Rat's consent,*
> *I couldn't marry the president,*
> *ah ha, ah ha, woo hoo!"*

I can remember waiting at the screen door for my hero, my Daddy, to arrive home from work. There was little breeze in that little house in the summer, and my Mother wore short shorts while teaching herself to cook from what she called "The Bible according to Betty Crocker".

On Saturday mornings or late summer evenings Dad and I would park ourselves on the front porch and watch the cars zip by on Highway 7, and we'd play memory.

"What kind of car is that one?" he'd say.

"A '57 Chevy."

"What about the red one?"

"A Ford."

"What about my car?"

"A jalopy."

"You're a bright girl, Pauline. In life you're gonna have to use that head; it's more than a hat-rack."

In the back yard my Father made me the "biggest swing in the world". It hung suspended by about twenty feet of rope on the mature limb of an old willow tree. It had a long wooden seat he'd painted red. It was cooler in the shade, and the swinging motion lent a breeze. I sat beside him and hung onto his every word.

"You know, Molly Mouse, castles in Ireland touch the sky. When I was a young lad, my family lived on an estate called Monkstown Farm. At the back of our house was this apple orchard. In the spring, when the trees were in blossom, there would be a sweet smell in the air. There was this stone wall around the orchard with broken glass at the top so no little buggers like us could get in and rob the apples when they were ripe. There we'd be, a gang of kids standing quietly near the garden wall, shushing each other to listen to the buzz of the bees."

"Your Granddad worked two jobs to keep the bread and butter on the table. When we were little, he'd bath us in a wash-tub by the fire on a Saturday night. He'd give us a polish and trim our hair and nails. He's a good and decent man."

"My brother Pat is the eldest. He is married now. His wife's name is Gwen, and they have a young lad about your age. Pat always loved opera music and photography. Then came your Auntie Theresa, your Godmother, who lives here. When we were kids, she liked film stars and swimming. Next came my sister Maureen. She and I were joined at the hip, "Oxo and Alo, the Bisto Kid's." Maureen is married and lives in England with her husband Harry and their son Thomas. I have a sister, Dara, that I sent on a trip down the stairs in a suitcase once, and she chipped her tooth. You have an Auntie Kate who is very bold. When she was a girl she went wee-wee in a basket of apples, and then gave them out to the kids on the street. Next was Moira. She was your Grandad's pet because she had red hair. Daddy would say to her, 'Come here, me little red hen.' We called my little brother Peter, Padder. He went to heaven when he was seven, and that was very sad. Brenna and Maggie are the babies; they're still at home with my mother, your Granny Kiely. When she wasn't washing up, she was peeling spuds for a stew. The woman is the salt of the earth. When we'd fight, she'd cool us off with a bucket of water."

"Why did you leave your home, Daddy?"

"I had to, to find your mother and make you. Don't worry, Mousey. Someday I'll take you to Ireland and you can catch a leprechaun."

"Dad?"

"Ya."

"I'm not a mouse, you know. I'm a girl."

"That you are."

Chapter Two

49 Sherwood Forest Drive

T here were rain drops on the windshield of the pick-up truck my Father borrowed the damp dark Friday night that we moved ourselves into the brand new house on Sherwood Forest Drive. All their worldly possessions didn't amount to much more than a couple of loads. I was a curious three-year-old that Dad called "Big Ears", and I remember sitting between him and my Mother on the truck's bench seat, my head moving back and forth like the wipers, attempting to follow the conversation. Heaven forbid I'd miss anything.

The Kielys were the proud owners of the right half of a solid brick, semi-detached home. It cost about eighteen grand in 1964 for a semi like ours in Markham. It was a back-split raised bungalow that my Father called 'a postage stamp' because all these houses were the same. I played hop-scotch on the black and white kitchen floor that was tiled like a checker board. My Mom couldn't believe there were two bathrooms. All the walls had been painted egg shell white, with the exception of their bedroom which was violet. When showing people the house, Dad called his room "The Purple Passion Room" or "Conception Headquarters". He had made their white bed frame, headboard, and dresser.

The subdivision was built on a hill, and our street had a steep grade. The lawns were still mud. From the front picture-window we watched families move in all around us. A German family, the Strollenbergs, already lived on the north side of our house. They had four boys, three Volkswagons, and two rodents. Mrs. Strollenberg was a plump and jolly lady, much older than my Mom. She wore her grey hair in a bun, and cotton dresses with an apron. You'd hear her accent when she called, "Teddy, Johnny, Eddie, or Bobbie!" Bobbie shared her Avon lipstick samples with me.

Across the street, Nuala and Tom Garry had three boys, Sean, Aidan, and Tim. Nuala had an infectious laugh and radiant smile. Her "Tommy" didn't have much to say. He was a proud man that appeared to be taking it all in. There must have been a sale on brush cuts, cow licks, and blue eyes at the Garry's because all three boys had them. The Hinton's lived next door to the Garry's. They had a teenage daughter, and a freckle-faced son named Kevin that was my age.

The days grew longer. The houses filled up, and rolls of sod vacuumed up the mud. Most Sundays my Father would pick up Auntie Theresa at Yonge and Finch, and bring her and her chocolate bars home for afternoon tea. Auntie Theresa worked at Rowntrees. She had a front tooth that was half capped in gold, and she did Irish dancing. Some Sundays Herself and her Kit Kat bars or Black Magic Chocolates, or both, arrived in Grand-dad's Buick with young Seamus and Caroline.

There we'd all be with a big pot of tea, biscuits, and sandwiches on the table. In a puff of smoke a thin cross-legged Granddad Kiely was sporting his mug while seated at the chrome table's end. He'd nod towards his burning cigarette and announce, "These things are killing me."

My Father started moonlighting for extra money, doing odd jobs on the side. In a daze in the morning he would shut off his alarm, and doze off back to sleep. Then, as if struck by lightning, he'd wake with a jolt, hit the ground running, and show up at the job. Late!

Mr. Wade noticed. Dad had a solution; he would put the alarm clock in the kitchen. That way he'd have to go downstairs to turn it off, and by then he'd be awake.

The next morning we didn't wake up to the alarm clock. We all woke with a jolt to someone pounding on our front door. Dad jumped up to answer it. A man said, "Good morning. My name is Al James. I moved in next door over the weekend. My wife and I were wondering if there was any particular reason why you blare your radio out your kitchen window at six a.m., sir?"

"I've been having trouble getting up in the morning, and thought it might help if the alarm was in another room," Dad said.

"Well, I'm not sure how that's working for you. But the Missus and me, and our four kids, have been up for over an hour now, thanks to your racket; and we've witnessed no indication of life over here."

"The name's John Kiely." Dad said, and he stuck out his hand for a shake. "I'm sorry for the trouble. It won't happen again." The door closed. My Father's face turned red. His bed-head hair was sticking up like an Iroquois' as he rain-danced chanting, "Shit, shit, shit, late again".

Al and Beryl James were in their early thirties. This was a second marriage for Beryl, a little lady with a rowdy laugh. Mr. James wore tortoise-shell-rimmed glasses; he had dark hair around a bald spot. He was generally polished, modelling the suits he sold for Simpsons. He also worked two jobs, driving limo part-time. She'd had three children, Debbie, Jimmy, Beth, and "they" had Wanda; but you'd never know because they were just one big happy family.

Dark-haired Debbie was in high school, loved the books, and babysat me sometimes. Jimmy had big feet. He ate ice cream by the carton, and in his spare time he drove the family sedan twenty feet up and down their driveway. Blonde Beth wore big bell bottoms, and blew pink bubbles. Beth was into music, and she walked me to kindergarten at Robinson Public

School. Sometimes we'd eat apples as we cut through the park, or listen to "The Byrds", *Turn, Turn, Turn,* on her transistor radio. Little Wanda had ringlets of gold. In a game I called 'barber', I chopped them off with garden shears as she sat on a stool amongst the tools, oil, and car parts in Bobby Strollenberg's garage.

I was four, and much bigger than Wanda; sometimes she sunk her teeth into me in defence. Our Mothers did crafts. They made us funny dolls they called "Gonks". Beryl said, "Children go through phases." She and Nuala were my Mom's best friends. Nuala wasn't always able to join them when they took upholstery workshops, typing, and yoga classes. She was up to her arse in kids.

Dinner at our house was served at six prompt. It generally consisted of meat in the form of a chicken leg, or pork chop, or hamburger, with potatoes, usually mashed, and a serving of previously frozen peas with cubed carrots, or corn on the side. I never complained; it was cooked with love and served hot.

After the evening meal two level teaspoons of sugar went plip, plop, into his cup. Then the teaspoon went *ting, tang,* off its sides as he blended the strong tea with milk and sugar. We talked about our day, and one thought would lead to another which usually led to a story about the *Old Country*. I was glad I had big ears.

"My granddad Kiely, your granddad's daddy, had this pony he called Bubbles. I stayed with him the summer I was thirteen. The old fella and I would clip-clop into Dublin with the pony and trap to collect broken biscuits and old bread from the bakeries for his pigs. My granddad had a small farm in Dun Lougheire. The man never swore, nor drank, nor smoked. Whenever he lent my father Bubbles and the trap on a Sunday, he'd shake a bony finger at him and say, 'If I ever see that mare tethered outside a pub, it will be the last day you lot will have a loan of her.'"

This one day we were on our way home, Bubbles' hooves beating a rhythmic clip-clop-clip-clop when we went right through an intersection. My Granddad had dozed off; so I elbowed him and said, 'Granddad, we're after going through a stop sign.' And he says, 'No bother, John, Bubbles knows her way home.' It would be near dark by the time we got back to DunLaoghaire, and while I did chores he'd cook up a pair of chickens, one each. We et them, and then we'd wash up in what was left of the tea, too tired to go out and fetch clean water."

Tony Kiely with Granddad Kiely and Bubbles 1950

There were lots of kids to play marbles, tag, ball, or skip with on Sherwood Forest Drive: Maryanne, Ellen, Kevin, Sean, Bobby, Wanda, and me. Most days we all got along; a few times I'd stomp home pissed off because that Sean Garry sang his song to the beat of the Adams Family chorus;

"The Kiely family started,
when Mr. Kiely farted.
That's why they're all retarded,
the Kiely family.
Da da da dumb, da da da dumb."

To this day Sean Garry remembers the time I didn't stomp home, but knocked him down, sat on his chest, and was giving it to him, screaming "Shut up, just shut up!" until his mother pulled me off.

I barely but do remember the night that a dark-haired man with Buddy Holly glasses came to our door. He carried a brief case, and said he was with Allstate - *The Good Hands People.* This man was invited into our living room, and promptly served a cup of coffee. His brief case popped open, and he passed my parents papers to have a look at. His words aimed for the heart. "Now, Mr. Kiely, should something unforeseen happen to you, what would become of your wife and your child? Who would look after them? There are elements of danger in your line of work, and I wouldn't want to see your family put out on the streets because you chose not to purchase life insurance today."

My Dad said, "Mister, I invite you to take a good hard look at my wife. I am without a doubt, sir, that should something unforeseen happen to me, there'd be a line-up at the door ready to take her in, even with a child. I'm sure she'd pan out just grand without me."

The Allstate man said, "I can't argue with that", and the two of them shook hands before Dad closed the front door.

Mom said, "Your Father got to thinking about it, and phoned that man a couple of weeks later to purchase a small policy."

It was a gorgeous summer day and I wasn't very old when my Mother said, "You stay here. I'm just going up there to dive off the diving board and I will be right back." We were at a sandy beach that had a dock in the water with a diving board. I could reach the dock on the shallow side, but when I tried to go around it to watch my Mom go off the diving board, the water dropped off suddenly and I was over my head. It was a near death experience. I saw light and could see my foot kicking but not reaching the rocks deeper down. Some boys were waiting in line for my Mother to jump or dive or do something, and then one noticed me and said, "Hey, lady, isn't that your kid?" Two boys must have figured out that I was in real trouble because they jumped in and each took an arm and towed me to shore. My frazzled Mother was upset with me. My Father said my punishment was that I had to stay out of the water for the rest of the day. Mom never did get to dive off that diving board.

We rushed around most Sunday mornings to get to St. Patrick's late, or just in the nick of time. Peter from the Texaco station asked my parents to stand in as godparents for his little girl Christine. There was just him and the Mrs. All their family was in Portugal. I was still four. After the ceremony the parish priest, Father Culnan, leans over and whispers to me, "I think that baby looks a bit like your Dad." And I said, "I think that baby looks more like you."

It was a week day the day I'd been playing with Kevin Hinton, and could see my Mother in her white shorts standing with her arms folded, leaning against our front door frame. At the curb there were two parked cars. I walked between them, and looked at my Mother to give me the nod to cross. From her angle it was all clear; so I stuck my head out. From nowhere this rust bucket full of buddies, with its chrome bumper hanging, clipped me and knocked me down, and out.

When I came to, I was on a gurney in the back of a station wagon ambulance. My face was scraped and bruised, and I held my cut index finger high in the air. The police had gotten their statements, and some neighbours were still hanging around when Dad arrived on the scene.

Mom said, "Your Father looked in on you, and then at me, before he walked over to the young guy that was driving that car and grabbed him by the throat."

"You could've killed my daughter, you fuckin' eigit! Get out of my sight! And get that God damn shit-box fixed before you do manage to kill someone!" The policeman said that behaviour wasn't going to help matters. The paramedics cleaned me up, and I had to stay inside for a day or two. Apparently my Father had seen this car at Peter's just days before, and mentioned then that the bumper should be fixed.

Maryanne came to visit me. She gave me a white and navy blue basket filled with pennies. I had to give her gift back because Maryanne's sister had just given her the basket as a souvenir gift from Italy, and she got the pennies by emptying her piggy bank. Maryanne's grandparents lived with her or maybe she lived with them. They had a cuckcoo clock. She spoke softly, and had wispy blond hair and slate blue eyes. I was grateful for her friendship.

Three weeks after the car accident Mom and I were at the Tripps in Richmond Hill, the home of my Mother's sister, Agnes, and her husband Ross. He was the only person I allowed to call me "Paul". Depending on her mood, Auntie Agnes reminded me of either Olive Oil or Jackie Kennedy. They had two daughters, Patsy and Gail, and a son, Gary, who was a year older than me.

Gary and I would listen to his "Peter and the Wolf" record. We were allowed to make our own toast and smear it with homemade jams. It was entertaining being seated on stools at their table. His sisters whined when I chewed with my mouth open.

They had this nasty pinto pony named Amby, and a few chickens in their back garden. Once Amby had her bridle on, she was better. She sure was hard to catch. It was fun in the winter when Uncle Ross rigged up a contraption whereby he hooked a rope around the horn on Amby's saddle and a toboggan, and we dashed across the snow.

Once, in a closet Gary showed me his and I showed him mine. Another time he showed me his grandfather's pilot license that looked like a passport. Gary said his grandfather, Leonard Tripp, had lied about his age when he joined the army back in England during the First World War. He got trench foot, and was transferred to gunman on a plane. Apparently the man had

Len Tripp's Pilots licence- 1929

a knack for flying. After Len Tripp came to Canada he entered an Air Race at the Barrie Fair, and won. Orville Wright was the judge who issued the winner this special license.

I was coming down an old wooden slide in their back yard that Uncle Ross got for free because it had a split spot in the wood. The jagged wood caught my arm and tore it open. My Mother's chin dropped when I came around the side of the house with my bloody arm. Luckily Auntie Agnes had the car, and Donna Channella was home to look after the other kids. Auntie Agnes got towels and drove directly to the hospital. I passed out. When I came to, they were sewing up my arm, and my Mom was there. I heard my Dad's voice holler "Yoo-hoo," in the hall. I saw my Mom step through the door, where she fainted. A bright light was in my eyes when they were sewing up my arm.

A few days later I was burning up with fever. So Mom called Dr. Outread, and he came to 49 Sherwood Forest Drive on a Sunday night in the middle of the night. She said I was sleeping soundly in their bed when the good doctor pulled my nightie up, my knickers down, spanked my bum, and stuck me with a needle. I had blood poisoning and that antibiotic needle probably saved my life. I jumped and yelled, may have had a sip of water, and fell right back to sleep. We went to his office first thing in the morning, and I gave him the hairy eyeball. Then I was under a bright light again. Over a steel pan his skilled hand guided the knife that cut open the stitches, and then this green and yellow gunk spat out a sliver of wood.

One day my Dad went to Toronto but he didn't bring home Auntie Theresa; he brought home Aunt Kate, his sister Katherine. "The Wild One," he said, "had come by boat, and was as sick as a dog the entire journey."

Aunt Kate, and my Mother – 1963

She said to my Mother, "I saw the few snaps you sent me Ma after the wedding, and I thought to myself, 'Imagine an ordinary Joe like our John marrying a film star like that. I'm going to Canada.' So I've arrived."

Aunt Kate stayed with us. She had the look of Natalie Wood from "West Side Story". She had a white fringe bikini, and in no time landed a job in a factory called Amalgamated Electric that was within walking distance. Then she started to date this fella from work. The only trouble was her boyfriend, Jerry Clancy, fiancé actually, would be arriving from Ireland soon.

When Jerry arrived, my Father said he was stuck between a rock and a hard place. Aunt Kate got a basement apartment, and Jerry stayed with us. On the eve of what should have been Jerry's stag, my Dad had to tell him about Dave: Dave Spang, a spitting Canuck who sang about 'a girl wearin' nothing but a smile, and a towel, on the billboard of the big old highway': Dave Spang, the fella she'd met on the job, the one who grew up in a one horse town called Sunderland: Dave Spang, the one and the same who'd swept his sister right off her feet.

Jerry took things in stride. Aunt Kate explained she'd felt he was more like a brother. She said, "We'd been pals since we were kids, and never gone past second base." She also said, "Jerry is a handsome chap, and didn't he come to Canada for adventure. We can still be friends."

Aunt Kate lit the place up. She'd come down the stairs doing her exercise, "I must, I must, I must improve me bust. The bigger the better, the tighter the sweater, the boys will like me better!"

Or if my Father said, "Pull my finger", Aunt Kate would say, "Ah, now, a fart, a fart is just a gentle breeze that blows between my knees. It bursts the stitches in my britches, and suffocates the fleas".

She gave lessons on eyelash-batting and how to wiggle my arse when I walked. I adored her.

The next thing I knew we were going to Dr. Outread's because my Mother was having a baby. My Father was always singing:

"Oh, the baby's knuckle or the baby's knee,
Where will the baby's dimple be?
Baby's cheek or baby's chin,
Seems to me it would be a sin.
If it's always covered by a safety pin,
Where will the dimple be?"

Each month Mother and I would make the long walk to the plaza to the doctor's office, but we'd leave empty-handed because he only had boys, and they knew I wanted a girl. I was getting tired of going to this doctor who only had boys. One day I wouldn't put on my coat. My arms were dead, and I couldn't walk either. Mom forced on the coat, squeezed my wrist and made me walk. Her tummy was quite a size. We were cutting through an empty-lot short-cut where there was a big mud puddle. I just sat down in it and cried, "I don't want a baby. Why do we need a baby? Why do I have to walk to this doctor who doesn't have any girls anyway?"

I got my wish for a girl because Colleen Joy Kiely was born January 2, 1966. I was told to call my Mother's mother, Memère. She came to stay with us to look after me and my Dad, and Mom, when she and my sister came home. Mom says, "I asked your Father to bring me something to wear home from the hospital, and the ding-bat brings me a red cocktail dress I'd worn years ago to a New Year's Party. I couldn't wear that!" We had lots of visitors to see the baby.

Memère wore plain dresses. She was a smidgen of a thing with soft, white, shoulder-length hair. She hid her green eyes behind robin's-egg blue, cat's-eyes bifocals. Her cheekbones were high, her lips were full, but her teeth and boobs were false. My Mother says, "Our clothing was very fitted in those days. If you couldn't fill the bust line, then what God has forgotten, you can always stuff with cotton." Memère's skin was a creased hide.

My Mom and Colleen slept in most mornings. After cereal or an egg, me and Memère would hook rugs while we watched black and white television. I'd hold my hands about six inches apart, and she'd wind wool around them. Then she would feed the wool into a little machine that I churned like a jack-in-the-box. It clattered as it cut our wool into two inch lengths for the multi-coloured rugs. Memère smiled during Chez Hélène, a French puppet show; and I was in a trance when The Friendly Giant's low voice said, "Look up, way up, and I'll call Rusty," and then he'd whistle for Gerome the giraffe. She drank black coffee, rolled her own smokes, and thoroughly enjoyed a game of solitaire.

I asked my Mother, "What can you tell me about Memère?"

And she said, "Well . . . her parents were Anna and Gelinas Rancourt, and her mother was a seamstress. She is one of thirteen kids, and her name was Alice Rancourt before she married my father. She was born on November 26, 1905 and grew up in Bigwood. My mother told me she met my father when he was working on St. David's church. We have traced the Beaulieu side back to a marriage in Quebec City. The elders used to tell us about a brave Pierre Hudon Beaulieu who came from a village in France called Anjour. They said he may have been a stow-away, as there is no record of him until his marriage to Marie Gobiel, on July 13, 1676. My mother's people weren't far behind my father's. If they weren't on one of the Cartier ships, they were on Champlain's. We used to say if they weren't on the first boat, they were on the second.

My mother's people, the Rancourts, befriended the Ojibway. They travelled inland by water, and eventually came to settle amongst these Native peoples of Manitoulin Island. I'm sure the Indians kept them alive those first few winters.

When we were kids my mother would go into the back yard and catch a chicken. Then she'd stick it under her arm and wring its neck. In a couple of hours we were eating chicken. We had a big garden in the summer, and she would do down her vegetables, make pickles, and bake bread. She'd stay up nights sewing, making underwear and T-shirts out of flour bags. She would curl the girls' hair in rags. Apparently my father proposed at Christmas in 1923 right before he left for the bush camp; and they were married the following May when he returned.

"My mother and father lived with his parents Arthur and Eloise Beaulieu when they were first married, and then they got their own farm nearby. After her husband died things were hard for my poor mother. Luckily some of her family ended up in Noelville, which is the next village to Alban. Relatives would

Wreck Sale poster

visit sometimes, or we might find a partridge or a rabbit on the porch. People had large families back then; so most of us left home at fifteen and sixteen."

I remember my Memère's heavy sighs and her looking so content, sitting on our sofa in the den. Aunt Kate looked like Queen Victoria the day Jack Kiely gave her away to Dave Spang. She was the only daughter out of his seven that he walked down the aisle.

My grandfather stopped visiting our house; so we visited him at his apartment in Willowdale. I remember a strange smell in the room as I stood at the edge of his bed. Granddad offered me some Quality Street Chocolates. The purple ones were his favourite.

He whispered to my Father. I was whooshed into the sitting room, and Dad said, "Don't look"; but I did, and I saw him carry his father down the hall in his arms, like a groom carries a bride. They went into the washroom. There wasn't much left of this fifty-six-year-old-man when he returned to the *Old Country* that Christmas.

Marilyn Munroe was through in August of `62, and John F. Kennedy in November of '63. Jack Kiely died on Irish time, on Irish soil, on January 19, 1966. He was a man who had done his best, but drew his last and final breath. My Father said he was never the same after the car accident, and figured the impact of the steering wheel on his chest triggered the cancer. My Dad said, "We know not the day, nor the hour, but death comes to us all like a thief in the night."

Neither Auntie Theresa nor Dad could afford to return to Ireland for their father's funeral. Caroline and Seamus were said to have been there, but they've never been seen or heard from since.

Maryanne, Bobby, and Kevin stayed at Robinson Public, but I got traded to the Catholic school for grade one. The good news was that that brat, Sean Garry, would be in my class. The first thing that greeted me and Mom when we entered the halls of St. Patrick's were big letters on a poster that read, "LSD

Kills". I could walk to school on my own. I was safe because the crossing guard at Highway 7, was a relative of the Mayor.

Once there was a man sitting in his car who asked me if I knew where Friar Tuck Way was? This was Sherwood Forest; sure, I knew. He motioned for me to come over to his car window because he couldn't hear me; and when I did, he had his zipper down, and his hand in his lap. He asked me to touch it, and I ran home as fast as I could. I never told my Mom, because one other time I told her about a boy babysitter who'd covered my mouth, and humped on me with our clothes on. He was crushing me. I was scared and couldn't breathe. Mom got angry and said, "Don't tell lies. Nobody likes a liar." So I didn't tell those lies anymore.

Our family would drive out to Swiss Chalet Park on a Sunday, and my Father would run and hurdle picnic tables, sometimes four or five in a row. In the winter he made a skating rink in the back yard, and a giant Gumby snowman in the front yard. Some boys came to the door asking, "Can Mr. Kiely come out and play?"

Once at Halloween he asked a boy, "Trick or Treat?"

The kid didn't answer, so Dad said, "Trick!" and put a small chicken bone in his Unicef box.

That kid was Steven from my class, and that's how I heard about it.

There was peace, love, and flower power protests on the news; and there was sex, and drugs, and Rock n' Roll. Ed Sullivan introduced all the new acts on his "Really Big Show". My parents enjoyed a good social on a Saturday night: Kate, Dave, Agnes, Ross, Bernice, George, Oscar, Lise, Al, Beryl, Nuala, Tom, and Jerry with his new girlfriend Donna, and voila, it's a party.

One Sunday morning I was jumping on their bed. I was laughing and singing, "I had Coke, I love Coke."

My Mom rolled over and said, "John, where did she get Coke? We ran out of mix last night."

So Dad says, "Let me smell your breath."

I blew on him and he said, "Shit, she's drunk. She must have drunk the dregs people left in their glasses. Molly Mouse, come in here and have a rest. Come on in here, pet, and I'll mind you."

My dark hair was long and usually tied back in a pony tail. My body had a habit of chubbing out before stretching up. My Dad said I was a brick shit-house, and I knew he meant it in a loving way. I never thought much about how I looked. I had brown hair, and brown eyes, and figured all the really pretty girls had blonde hair and blue eyes like Maryanne. Dad was glad I was tough enough to keep up with him when we'd go for our long walks around car lots. He loved cars, Fords and Chevys, especially the convertibles.

One day he came home in a banana yellow Mercury Marquis. It had black leather interior and a black rag-top roof, with power windows and locks, and headlight lids that flipped up. Mom had Colleen in the bathtub; she was nearly two. He was working on my Mother about buying this car, and was out on a test drive. Dad says to me, "Go out and hop in. Check her out." I did, and for the life of me after the door closed and the lights went out, I couldn't figure out how to get out. He must have had to do some talking 'cause I was in there for what felt like forever, and was just about to panic when he came out and said, "Go on inside. I have to take her back." That car was parked in our driveway less than two weeks later, and Mrs. James was determined to teach my Mother how to drive it. In that car I overheard my Mom tell her friend she thought she was expecting again.

Chapter Three

Sean, Sean, the Leprechaun

The joint was rocking in 1965 thanks to Beatlemania and The British Invasion! This generation were birth-control-pill-test-dummies. My Mother told me about one particular party they had been invited to. "It was this toga party. I'd never heard of a toga party. So there we are wearing sheets, and the women are all over your Father. I notice some men sizing me up; and I said, 'John Kiely, this ain't my kinda party. You can stay here, but I'm going home', and I started walking. He caught up with me a couple of blocks away. We went home together."

Dad said, "Your Mother was a fuddy-duddy who only liked to party with her family."

And Mom said, 'My family doesn't put the coochie-maulie hold on me."

Over tea Dad told me his carpentry apprenticeship began at the age of fourteen when he was 'The Nipper' on the job in the *Old Country* with his Da. The Nipper was the go-boy that fetched things, held things, and made the tea. As The Nipper, he was paid a pittance, and tipped a few cigarettes. But he learned things, like how to measure and cut lumber, and how to sweep up. "A gentle man named Mr. Macken was in charge on the job-site. He had this habit of saying, 'Ah, now, some t'ings can't be helped.' I was working away with my buddy, Morgan Mooney; and I says to Morgan, 'I bet you I can get Mr. Macken to say 'some t'ings can't be helped.' Then I took my hammer and deliberately smashed a pane of glass. Morgan said nothing. Mr. Macken came into the room, looked about, and asked, 'What's happened here?' And I said, 'I'm sorry sir, my hammer, it just slipped!' And says he, 'There, there, now lad. Some t'ings can't be helped."

My Father had his share of side work lined up these days. He would have been weighing the pro's and con's of going into business on his own. I can quote my old man more than once. "Didn't I find twenty bucks at the airport when I arrived in this land of opportunity, and she's been good to me ever since."

After guzzling a few cold ones, my Dad just started singing: sometimes Irish ballads, rebel songs, or funny ones like Roger Miller's, *You Can't Roller Skate in a Buffalo Herd*. I used to wonder how he remembered all the words. I figured they must have played 'Memory' a lot in Ireland because on Christmas day my Grandad Kiely would entertain his children by reciting by heart this entire Robert Service poem, *The Cremation of Sam McGee*:

> "There are strange things done in the midnight sun
> By the men who moil for gold;
> The Arctic trails have their secret tales
> That would make your blood run cold;
> The Northern Lights have seen queer sights,
> But the queerest they ever did see
> Was that night on the marge of Lake Lebarge
> I cremated Sam McGee.

> Now Sam McGee was from Tennessee,
> where the cotton blooms and blows.
> Why he left his home in the South to roam
> 'round the Pole, God only knows.
> He was always cold, but the land of gold

seemed to hold him like a spell;
Though he'd often say in his homely way
    that he'd "sooner live in hell".
On a Christmas Day we were mushing our way
    over the Dawson trail.
Talk of your cold! through the parka's fold
    it stabbed like a driven nail.
If our eyes we'd close, then the lashes froze
    till sometimes we couldn't see;
It wasn't much fun, but the only one
    to whimper was Sam McGee.
And that very night, as we lay packed tight
    in our robes beneath the snow,
And the dogs were fed, and the stars o'erhead
    were dancing heel and toe,
He turned to me, and "Cap," says he,
    "I'll cash in this trip, I guess;
And if I do, I'm asking that you
    won't refuse my last request."
Well, he seemed so low that I couldn't say no;
    then he says with a sort of moan:
"It's the cursed cold, and it's got right hold
    till I'm chilled clean through to the bone.
Yet 'tain't being dead — it's my awful dread
    of the icy grave that pains;
So I want you to swear that, foul or fair,
    you'll cremate my last remains."
A pal's last need is a thing to heed,
    so I swore I would not fail;
And we started on at the streak of dawn;
    but God! he looked ghastly pale.
He crouched on the sleigh, and he raved all day
    of his home in Tennessee;
And before nightfall a corpse was all
    that was left of Sam McGee.
There wasn't a breath in that land of death,

and I hurried, horror-driven,
With a corpse half hid that I couldn't get rid,
    because of a promise given;
It was lashed to the sleigh, and it seemed to say:
    "You may tax your brawn and brains,
But you promised true, and it's up to you to
    cremate those last remains."
Now a promise made is a debt unpaid,
    and the trail has its own stern code.
In the days to come, though my lips were numb,
    in my heart how I cursed that load.
In the long, long night, by the lone firelight,
    while the huskies, round in a ring,
Howled out their woes to the homeless snows
    — O God! how I loathed the thing.
And every day that quiet clay
    seemed to heavy and heavier grow;
And on I went, though the dogs were spent
    and the grub was getting low;
The trail was bad, and I felt half mad,
    but I swore I would not give in;
And I'd often sing to the hateful thing,
    and it hearkened with a grin.
Till I came to the marge of Lake Lebarge,
    and a derelict there lay;
It was jammed in the ice, but I saw in a trice
    it was called the "Alice May".
And I looked at it, and I thought a bit,
    and I looked at my frozen chum;
Then "Here", said I, with a sudden cry,
    "is my cre-ma-tor-eum."
Some planks I tore from the cabin floor,
    and I lit the boiler fire;
Some coal I found that was lying around,
    and I heaped the fuel higher;
The flames just soared, and the furnace roared

— such a blaze you seldom see;
And I burrowed a hole in the glowing coal,
    and I stuffed in Sam McGee.
Then I made a hike, for I didn't like
    to hear him sizzle so;
And the heavens scowled, and the huskies howled,
    and the wind began to blow.
It was icy cold, but the hot sweat rolled
    down my cheeks, and I don't know why;
And the greasy smoke in an inky cloak
    went streaking down the sky.
I do not know how long in the snow
    I wrestled with grisly fear;
But the stars came out and they danced about
    ere again I ventured near;
I was sick with dread, but I bravely said:
    "I'll just take a peep inside.
I guess he's cooked, and it's time I looked";
    . . . then the door I opened wide.
And there sat Sam, looking cool and calm,
    in the heart of the furnace roar;
And he wore a smile you could see a mile,
    and he said: "Please close that door.
It's fine in here, but I greatly fear
    you'll let in the cold and storm —
Since I left Plumtree, down in Tennessee,
    it's the first time I've been warm."

There are strange things done in the midnight sun
By the men who moil for gold;
The Arctic trails have their secret tales
That would make your blood run cold;
The Northern Lights have seen queer sights,
But the queerest they ever did see
Was that night on the marge of Lake Lebarge
I cremated Sam McGee."

Dad said, "American films were all the rage back home. Sure we went mad jiving in the aisles the nights they showed "Blackboard Jungle" and "Jail House Rock" at the Savoy. Elvis may be *The King,* but the song *Shake Rattle and Roll* by Bill Hailey and the Comets will always be my favourite. Even if my Da hadn't immigrated I may have found me way to Canada. My dreams couldn't be reached in Ireland with the class distinction; there was no room for my wingspan over there. As a young lad I knew I wanted a wife and family, and hoped to be able to provide for them. There's plenty of money to be had here, and it's as good in my pocket as somebody else's."

He admired Canada's youth, energy, and natural resources. He was a race horse out of the gate. "Does it get any better than driving along with the top down on the wide open highway, with Chuck Berry singing *No Particular Place to Go?* He admired how anything was possible, and how different cultures and religions lived harmoniously compared to 'The Troubles' back home. Belfast was a bad scene: bombings, shootings, reports of civilians shot while sleeping in their beds.

The Irish have a way of saying "Da" softly with endearment. It is short for Dad, and indicates a closeness, like "of course you understand, because you're me Da". In Canada "Da" is sort of the start of the word "dumb" like "duh" and indicates "Whoops, I've made a mistake".

Sometimes we went to Toronto for a Sunday drive, and ended up at Mass at St. Mike's where my Father said, "The flags of the world all pray under one roof . . .I'd say he likes that, God, I mean."

Canada was filling up with new Canadians from all walks of life. Toronto had its districts of different nationalities. Most people managed speaking their own dialect of English. It was of a certain Irishman's opinion that if you were of German decent you had *a square head;* if you were of Dutch background you had *a wooden head;* Blacks were *Black,* French were *Frogs,* Brits were *Limeys,* and most of them were *"Limey Bastards!"* The people from Portugal were *Pork Chops,* and all nationalities of Asia were simply labelled *Chinamen*. My Father told me that Confucius says, "Man who go to bed with itchy bum, wake up with stinky finger."

He also told me, "In Ireland you only find Irish people; and for the most part, there are those who are Irish, and those that wish they were." He said this in jest, but repeated it often enough that I almost believed him. In my mind all the nations of the world knew of his Ireland, and could only hope or dream of having the great fortune of being born in this magical place. In time I came to understand that he was simply born, baptised, and sworn into this mindset by his proud people; and he does come from a land of legends and folklore. Even at an early age I found it tough to draw lines between different heritages. When I looked around me I didn't see Catholics or Protestants. I didn't see Black people, or Chinamen, or Jews. What I saw was a classroom of Canada's smorgasbord of nations. Everyone knew where they came from, but it wasn't important. We knitted together the way kids find a way to do.

A drunk person tends to repeat himself. A drunk person doesn't listen to what other people say, or else doesn't hear them. A person coasting on a few drinks is usually funny. A drunk person who is loud and obnoxious is no fun. I remember him sometimes drunk with a hangover, sleeping past noon the next day, and holding his head that was full of remorse. I didn't like it when my Dad got drunk. It didn't happen all that often. Though there was the time I made them breakfast in bed. I was proud of the pair of fried eggs and toast I had made by myself, but my hung-over Father threw his plate at the wall. My Mother said she needed roller skates to keep up with him and his moods. She said, "I knew I'd married an Irishman. I just didn't know I'd married the country."

The story was always the same at the end of a drinking session; he smelled, his complexion was flushed, his hair was a mess, and he sat in a heap behind a bunch of empty beer bottles that he called 'dead soldiers'.

"Me Da tried to bring the lot of us to Canada years before the three of us immigrated. That plan was somehow bolluxed, bang-jackxed; you know, just fecked. Then Padder got sick with the leukemia; and God bless us, he died. After that things were never the same at home. Mammy went a bit mad, and Da wouldn't come home till all hours. There wasn't much sleep in the house. She was up half the night hunting for the *riff-raff* under our beds, and staring at the locks and bolts on the doors. He swung a hammer all day, and drove a taxi for Uncle Joe evenings and weekends. I remember this night when my Ma had my Da by the short end of his tie, and she was choking him. And there's me Da all red in the face saying, 'Let go, let go of me, woman. You'll be the death of me.'"

"And my mother's raised voice saying, 'Go on, go on then . . . go to the filthy pub, and yer stay-blonde trollop.'"

"When my father drove away, my mother would need a walk. She'd leave Theresa, Alo, or me in charge. Poor Mammy had no one to talk to. When she was nine years of age her own mother had died of T.B. The woman was only forty. The saddest thing there was she had just given birth to twins, and then the T.B. took them, plus a sister Brigitte, who was thirteen. Shortly after Brigitte died, her eldest sister, Winifred, contacted meningitis; and she died at seventeen years of age. Within a year and a half my mother lost five members of her family."

"Mammy had been close to the Grandmother Kiely, but sadly this friend too passed away in January of '46. When my mother returned she would tell us she'd walked half way to Dublin to cool off before lighting a candle in a chapel somewhere."

"There were happier days, true enough, when my parents went to the pictures. One time I told the little ones, 'I bet I can make it snow. We'll say a little prayer over here by the window,' and I said, 'Close your eyes, and keep them closed, and keep praying till I tell you to open them.'"

"So there's Kate, Moira, Brenna, and Dara, like little angels kneeling and praying by the window, and I'm climbin' the stairs sayin' 'Pray, pray louder'. I open the second story window, and shook feathers out of a pillow and shouted down, 'Open your eyes.' and the girls went on, 'Ahh John, 'tis snowing, 'tis lovely. Would you look at that.'"

Jack, Elizabeth, and Joe Kiely - 1930's

"When me parents came home to their front garden covered in feathers I was scolded, and punished. The next day I was to clean up the garden with no dinner. There I was working away, with me stomach turnin' when I heard, psssst, pssst! It was Maureen from up in the bedroom window. 'John, John', says she, and she lowers a package wrapped in brown paper by a string. It was a sandwich. She always was my favourite. Me and Maureen looked out for one another, and Theresa and Pat looked out for one another."

I took in a lot of information during tea time, like how "Maureen and Pat will never forget a fine May day in 1952. Maureen was around fourteen at this time, and she was asked would she serve as a tour guide for Uncle Joe? He gave her and Pat instructions to look smart, and meet him at the Royal Marine Hotel. Uncle Joe's taxi was a luxury car with plush bench seats that faced each other in the back. Uncle Joe pulled up to the curb and his window came down. He casually said, 'Maureen, hop in.' So she did, and there she found herself face to face with the most famous and popular comedy acts, Hollywood screen stars, Mr. Stan Laurel and Mr. Oliver Hardy. Maureen said, "I couldn't get over that Mr. Laurel's hair was really ginger, and Mr. Hardy was quite bald. They were nice fellows."

Joe Kiely with Stan Laurel and Oliver Hardy – 1952

Colleen was still in diapers on Valentine's Day in 1966 so she probably doesn't remember, but I do. Dad came in through the side door and called us to come down. He had his work boots and coat off, and was seated in a chair. The room smelled of saw dust and a day's work. He motioned for my Mother to sit on his knee so she did. He kissed her, then scooped up Colleen and motioned for me to hop up and sneak a cheek with my sister.

He said, "Today my heart was so full! Am I the luckiest man on the planet? I have a gorgeous wife, and two lovely daughters."

Out of his breast-pockets came two little clear plastic hearts, filled with cinnamon hearts; one for me, and one for Colleen. He undid his shirt, and pulled out a heart made of wood with the words *I Love You* written in pencil, and said, "For Yolande." Then they started singing *Because I Don't Have a Wooden Heart.*

The Strollenburg's rodents were a ferret and snake. Before going asleep I sometimes worried about them getting loose, and finding their way into my room. I was given a dog for protection. A white Maltese Terrier. "He's an Italian dog named Pixie from *Louie the Wop.*"

My Dad even had *Louie the Wop* written in his phone book. I don't believe he ever just referred to Louie, a machine operator, without the tag line, *the Wop!*

He said, "You take a gob of shit in one hand, and a gob of shit in the other, and when you slap your hands together it goes Wop." Dad loved *Louie the Wop*, and said he was "a good shit".

I never met the man, but this dog he gave me ate spaghetti, and barked like a rooster. It was a white hairball that skidded across the grass with its tail flapping. It crowed. It didn't bark. In this dog's mind 'Pixie' must have meant 'ferocious'. Or my dog must have been missing the size ratio in his genetics. Seriously it was a stellar performance aimed straight for the ankle of his prey. Why I say "my" is because I got to feed him, and I walked and watered him, and I had to go look for him, and call him with a pocket full of *Milk Bones* when he took off, apparently looking for action.

My Mother insisted, "Get that dog fixed!"

Whatever they fixed, he sure was better at staying home. Pixie was a cute little thing that loved Colleen, and riding in the car. Sometimes my sister and my dog were both tied to the clothes line. A few times the mailman knocked on our front door with bandaged fingers, complaining that when he slipped the envelopes through the slot, our dog nipped his fingers. And I believe him because sometimes the mail was ripped to bits. Once my Mother walked in on Colleen shaking out the contents of a box of *Corn Flakes* on her kitchen floor because, "Me and Pixie are hungry." And Colleen would say, "It's alright if dogs lick their bums, 'cause Mom says it's alright, right Mom?" And Mom would say "Right." But I wouldn't let Pixie lick his bum and lick my mouth. Colleen even let Pixie lick her ice cream. My dog slept with my sister.

One day Mrs. James came to our door wearing a crash helmet. She was with Wanda and Beth, and said, "I'm here to teach your Mother how to drive." When they caught sight of each other they knocked their heads back laughing. Beth would mind us, and Colleen and Pixie would play in the backseat of the car during her lessons.

Beryl James says she'll never forget the day she took my Mother to Aurora to get her licence. "The man doing the testing asked Yolande to turn right and she turned left, and somewhere along the way she picked up a branch off a tree. But she passed. Somehow she passed and got her license. On the way home her knees were shaking, and she went snow white. So I said, 'Want an Aspirin?' and she took two." Nuala said she'd no desire whatsoever to be behind the wheel of a car.

My Mother had a pony tail that slept on her dresser. Her own hair was soft, and for special occasions she spent the day in rollers, but during the week she just stretched it back and clipped on her phoney pony tail. Her cooking was pretty good by now, as she'd had plenty of practice cause there was no filling up my Father's hollow leg. We had a French Provincial dining room suite. Aunt Kate and Uncle Dave would come over for dinner on Sundays.

Mom told me how when she first came to Toronto she watched television and listened to the radio to learn English. She picked it up quickly, and before long was working at a restaurant with her sister, Anne, near Massey Hall, downtown. "Imagine a little French girl from Alban, as fresh as anybody off the boat, serving a big star like Marty Robbins his order for 'A tall milk.'"

We had colour television now with rabbit ears that picked up three channels; so I wanted for nothing. But my parents wanted another baby; so they made one. Sean, Sean, the leprechaun, was born on Christmas Eve in 1967 - Canada's Centennial Anniversary. Dad had taken Mom to the Expo Exhibit held in Montreal that year. She'd travelled with "a bun in the oven."

If anyone asked my age at the hospital I was to say I was ten, and if I stood up straight we should get away with it. Sean was so tiny, and he had a little green knitted bell pinned on his chest, seeing as it was Christmas. My Dad sure was happy to have a son. He put a brand new hammer in the baby's bassinet, and the nurses told my Mother that was adorable. Dad was always singing, "Sean, Sean, the leprechaun, kissed the girls with nothing on." By the time his young lad was eighteen months his Daddy wasn't singing; instead only calling him 'the silent but deadly little bugger' because his son kept stealing the tubes out of their clock radio. He would hide them in the covers, or between the mattress and box spring, or in a shoe in the closet. Then 'that little bugger' couldn't or wouldn't tell you where he had put them. My little brother had long eye lashes, big feet, and fair hair. Apparently he was the image of my Father who had black hair! Sean slept lots and Dad worked lots.

Sean and Colleen Kiely - 1968

One time Sean found a nail and put it in an electrical socket, and did it go boom. The next time Nuala Garry came over 'the silent but deadly little bugger' had something to say, "Lula, the plug! The plug, Lula!"

The sugar went plip plop into his tea, and the spoon was going ting tang as he was stirring it when Dad announced, "I've been socking a little money aside. It's time we visit Ireland."He had a trip planned for September. Our best clothes were mended, washed, pressed, and packed. I was motivated to stick to the little diet my Mother put me on. We had to look our best. My Father was like a broken record that was stuck on this one song;

> And we're all off to Dublin in the green, in the green
> Where the helmets glisten in the sun
> Where the bayonets flash and the rifles crash
> To the rattle of a Thompson gun
>
> Oh I am a merry ploughboy and I ploughed the fields all day
> Till a sudden thought came to my head that I should roam away
> For I'm sick and tired of slavery since the day that I was born
> And I'm off to join the IRA, and I'm off tomorrow morn
>
> I'll leave aside my pick and spade, I'll leave aside my plough
> I'll leave aside my horse and yoke, I no longer need them now
> And I'll leave aside my Mary, she's the girl that I adore
> And I wonder if she'll think of me when she hears the rifles roar
>
> And when the war is over and dear old Ireland is free
> I'll take her to the church to wed, and a rebel's wife she'll be
> Well, some men fight for silver and some men fight for gold
> But the IRA are fighting for the land that the Saxons stole.
>
> (as sung by The Dubliners)

Since Sean was a baby, we got really good seats on the plane. Our ears popped on take-off but once we got settled, a stewardess took me up to the cockpit to meet our pilot, and see the switches and instrument panel, and all the gadgets it took to fly this plane. Harry Darcy would meet us at Heathrow Airport in England, and we'd stay with him and Maureen and the kids for a few days.

When we arrived at their north London, light blue, modular home, Dad put faces to the names I'd heard so many times. "This is your Auntie Maureen, Uncle Harry, and their children, Thomas, Sadie, and Declan." Thomas was a year older than me, Sadie a year older than Colleen, and Declan and Sean were about the same age. The adults shared what they called lemonade, out of a bottle labelled Canadian Club. Thomas and I were given a few shillings to get a paper and sweets.

I had never been in such a busy place. Tall dark buildings with big doors lined the sidewalks. Traffic lights blinked red, yellow, and green; and herds of little cars followed us, intersection after intersection. I couldn't see through the sea of backsides, as mostly adults walked before, beside, and around me. Thomas ran ahead and ducked into a doorway, and for a moment I was all alone in this strange city where everyone spoke funny. I must have passed him because he came up behind me and shouted, "Boo"! Then he and I went into a small dark shop where a bell tied over the door rang when we opened it. We got the paper for Uncle Harry, and a few bars of chocolate in exchange for big coins. I was relieved when we returned and were greeted by the wagging tail of their yellow Lab, Goldie.

Harry had work at the post office. Thomas had school. Auntie Maureen would mind Sadie, Sean, and Declan so that Dad, Mom, Colleen and I could do some sightseeing. The first day we toured London on red double-decker buses passing a clock named Big Ben, and the Queen's house – Buckingham Palace. We watched the changing of the guards. On day two, after we saw the Crown Jewels, London Bridge, and fed pigeons at Trafalgar Square, we had to pop back around to the house because Colleen and Mom were "knackered" which I knew meant exhausted.

After tea Dad was singing *England Swings* by Roger Miller, and he and I went for a stroll late in the afternoon. We ended up paying a visit to Madame Tussaud at her Wax Museum.

The place was amazing, full of life-sized figures of movie stars and famous people. Although they were still, they looked so perfect and real. Dad grabbed my hand when we entered the house of horrors where every scary beast or gruesome monster imaginable stared right through you.

After vivid images of fangs dripping with blood, guillotines chopping off heads, and Lizzy Borden hacking up her parents, we came to the exit. The likes of Béla Lugosi and Vincent Price had managed to scare the bejaysus out of me. I was in bad shape; so he bought me an ice cream to steady my nerves, but I still shook and my butterscotch scoop hit the sidewalk. When we returned my Auntie Maureen tucked me under her arm, and she said, "Jesus, John Kiely, are you mad all together? Look how you're after frightening this poor child."

We travelled by train through the night from Euston Station in London to Holly Head in Wales. I remember just about falling asleep when the train would blow its whistle, and lights would come on as we'd stopped at another station. It was a long night, and we caught the morning mail boat to Dun Laoghaire from Wales. Dad said we could walk to his mother's in nearby Dalkey from there.

Chapter Four

Blarney

I remember the sting of the scent of salt water when running down the ramp off the ferry when we arrived. Instead of walking all the way we caught the Number 8, a green double-decker bus. It deposited us at Bullock Harbour. I went down near the sea and picked up some shells because the tide was out.

We walked to my Granny's house along winding narrow sidewalks, with parked cars on the edges of the little roads. Most of the homes we passed were stucco semis with stone garden walls that retain passersby at the sidewalk. They had small driveways on either side. Fragrant roses in all colours were as big as my hand. Thick rose vines and mature holly and ivy covered the stone walls. Gardens were dotted with the odd palm tree. I didn't expect to see palm trees in Ireland. The forty shades of green were very luscious in September of 1968.

Sean was in the pram. Colleen was little, so she rode in the pram too. I walked, Mom pushed, and Dad carried our cases. He put them down and knocked on the door of 32 St. Beignets Villas. It swung open and there she was, my Granny, 'the swingingest Granny in town'. She wasn't old like some of my friend's Grannies. Her hair was auburn, she was strong and slim, and wearing a blouse and skirt. Her dark eyes were warm, and I could tell that she was well pleased to see her beloved son, and us too.

Her house was grey outside, and dark brown, mostly wood, on the inside. The bedrooms and bathroom upstairs had plaster walls that were a little brighter. Brenna and Maggie were at home. Brenna had my Father's colouring, raven black hair and sky blue eyes. At sixteen she was 'Twiggy' thin. Her hair and skirts were fashionably short, and she wore big bobble earrings. Her little sister, Maggie, had dimples and a shy smile. Her long hair was copper red and curly. She could easily have been a poster child for Ireland. A true Irish 'Colleen,' the Gaelic word for girl. We were served tea, ham and cheese sandwiches, plus warm scones that Maggie had baked in her cooking class.

I remember in the evenings when Maggie and Brenna were out, and before my parents went out, my Mom would say, "Colleen and Sean are dead to the world." I didn't like the sound of that. So I stayed close to Granny who was very alive rocking away by the fire. Once they were gone she set down her tea, and pulled a small package of what she called fags, but I knew to be cigarettes, out of her apron pocket. She struck a match, and thoroughly enjoyed that first haul.

"Well, young one, what do you have to say for yourself?"

I was seven. I didn't have much to say for myself.

She asked, "Cat got your tongue?"

I wondered, "What kind of a cat wants my tongue?"

"Your Father was a hellion as a lad, a little gurrier. Did he ever tell you that he dug a big hole in the garden, said he was building a swimming pool! Or that he hung a Neilson's ice cream sign on the side of the house this day, and the children were all knocking on that door looking for ice cream! I thought I was going mad all together. I had no ice cream, and himself and Maureen over the wall laughing their arses off. Ahh, now, fair play to him; so, wasn't he brilliant. Most of the others around here would be using newspaper and cardboard to fix the soles of their shoes, but wasn't it my John at the age of seven did a much better job using bits of rubber off old bicycle tires. Still he was the devil himself, indeed he was. He delivered turkeys at Christmas time on his bicycle for his Uncle Tommy. Jack's brother Tommy was the butcher in town. With the money John earned he treated this young one, Nora Riley, to the pictures. Wasn't poor Nora famous for falling asleep at the pictures, so sure enough she did. John had been counting on this, as he had a sausage that he'd nicked from the shop hidden in his pocket. Doesn't he carefully place it in her hand while she slept. When the lights turned up, and the poor child woke, didn't she scream bloody murder. It was the talk of the town. What could I do? Only send him to confession."

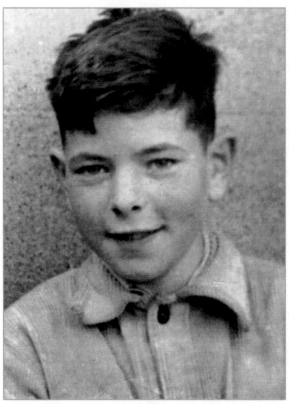

John Kiely - 1948

Granny would poke the fire, and go into sort of a trance staring at it. When she snapped out of the trance, she showed her age, with the bunions on her feet, and the varicose veins on her legs. Her knuckles were big and her hands were red. She lit another fag. There was comfortable silence before she spoke again.

"When I was a young one I thought I was special because I was always wearing me Sunday best and eating fancy sandwiches after riding in the funeral coach. After my sisters, and my mother died, sometimes I would run and run till I could run no more, and collapse in a heap, and cry myself to sleep in a field. Left standing after the T.B. went through the house was only Joe and Peggy, my father, and myself. It seemed a very short time before my father remarried."

"My stepmother didn't care for me so I was put out to sleep in the barn. When I was thirteen I was sent to Dublin to serve as a nanny to a wealthy family. They took me on trips to Cork and Kinsail. We travelled first class by train, and stayed in fancy hotels. I minded their three children, and in return they treated me as one of their own. These were glorious days, indeed. When my appendix near burst, wasn't it Mr. Jennings who paid for the operation and me stay at Hollis Street Hospital. Very good of him, he was under no obligation; sure, I was merely a servant. "The fire snapped and spat sparks, and she swept the glowing embers back into the grate.

"Do you remember your Granddad being in Canada then?"

"Yes," I said.

"Whatever became of Caroline?" she asked.

"I don't know."

"He would call for her at times nearer the end. T'is getting late, child. Maybe you better tuck-in for the night now."

We woke to fair skies and a feast of a full Irish breakfast: eggs, Hicks' sausages, black and white pudding, soda bread, and tea. The radio played jigs and reels Dad called diddley music. He said he was going for a walk, but he returned in a car. "I did walk to Dun Laoghaire to hire the car." So we packed this red VW beetle tight, and made arrangements with Mrs. Cunningham to keep an eye out for Maggie and Brenna. They were to go to Pat and Gwen for their tea.

I was more interested in what was going on inside the car than in what was passing by. I had to pay attention to follow the adult conversation, and I had never seen a stick shift, or ridden inside a bug. The car sort of hummed, and I remember a lot of head room in the bright tan interior.

Late afternoon we stopped at a pub to use the loo. Granny purchased a roasted chicken in a brown paper bag, and said she, "We're like a bunch of tinkers", as we tore apart and devoured the bird, tossing its bones and carcass out the windows. Granny, shifting her arse, asked, "Have you enough room, Pet?"

I winked at her when I answered, "I'd have more if you didn't come."

"Do you hear the cheek off this young one."

When we laughed, my parents caught on to our joke.

My Dad said, "Easy, Nelly, whoa, whoa girl, whoa," as he geared down to stop the car. We got out at Rock of Cashel Castle in Tipperary County. It was huge and impressive; and with it being the off season, there was no one else around. I slipped through a narrow entrance and climbed stone steps that went around and around and around. From the top window I called down to my family in the courtyard. They looked like ants down there. Dad said, "Jainey, that young one." and shouted, "Stay there, I'm coming up", so I did. From this viewpoint I took in rolling green fields outlined by stone walls and dotted with sheep.

Dad said, "This was the home of Brian Boru, the Druid King of Ireland."

We got dizzy descending the stone steps. We walked through the old graveyard with its proud and tall Celtic crosses, each encrypted with detailed carvings that told a story all their own.

We drove until dusk and found lodging at an inn in Cork. Once the kids were settled, the adults went downstairs for a few jars, and a bit of a sing-song. I slept with Granny, and the bed was damp in the morning because I'd had an accident. Granny said, "Pay no mind. We all make mistakes". So we squished back into 'the bug,' and did the bunk which meant we'd buzzed-off as quick as possible.

He beep-beeped the horn as we picked through flocks of sheep. I observed cattle and castles in pastures, and we passed the odd horse and caravan. Granny said, "Those people are the travellers; they're the unsettled people who travel from town to town tinkering with bits of work in exchange for some food or clothing. If you show them kindness, they'll bless you; if you don't, they've curses. So 'tis always wise to stay on their good side."

Soft rain had the road wet as we whipped around the round-a-bout on our way to Blarney Castle. Even in the off season there were other tourists here. When I was in line to bend back and kiss the sacred stone, Granny leaned over and whispered, "Why in heaven's name would you lot want to kiss that stone? Sure, don't the locals have a wee on it during the night."

Dad said, "Mammie, for Christ's sake, would you behave yourself. Here we are queued up to kiss the Blarney Stone with its *gift of the gab!* I sat down with my back to the stone wall. I was wearing a kilt, and there were black iron bars to hold onto as I leaned backwards to kiss a rock that a man pointed at. My Dad held my legs, and a local held my waist. Of course, everyone, including me, could see my knickers in the photograph.

When we returned to Dalkey, we had been invited to a tea at his brother Pat's. I was introduced to Auntie Gwen, and my cousins Kerry, Michael, and "the little babbey", Tess. We picked cabbage from the garden, and they had a pet tortoise. We played tag and hop-scotch on the walk. Uncle Pat had built a glass house in their garden for his wife's cacti.

My cousin Michael said, "You know Granny, right?"

And I nodded yes.

And he said, "She's mad all together. The other day we were waiting for the bus, and there was this lad selling newspapers. A well dressed woman walks past, and the lad says, 'Would you care to buy a paper, Mam?' Says she, 'What would I want with a paper? Sure I have a radio.' And Granny leans down and whispers to me, 'I'd like to see yer woman wipe her backside with that radio.' Isn't that mad?"

Granny Kiely - 1969

It is a strange thing with family. We were kids, who had never met before, but it was as if I'd known my Irish cousins all my life.

People and my parents seemed to be always coming and going while we were in Ireland. Granny and I found ourselves in each other's company hatching the fire during the evening on more than one occasion. Sparks snapped back at her when she tossed her butts into it. The hearth was large, but the cast iron grate was a regular size. The mantle and the clock upon it were mahogany, as was the wainscoting, stairs, and handrail. The lighting was dim but the room glowed warm, thanks to the company and the fire. There we found ourselves, me, just gone seven, and my Granny in the last year of her fifties, herself rocking in her rocking chair like it was any old day of the week. She wore a blue cardigan, a plain skirt and white blouse. The fire was illuminating the shine in her hair and her dancing black eyes when Granny asked, "Did you care for Caroline, then?"

I said, "Sure", because I did.

Granny mentioned that she had too many children, but couldn't be without a single one of them, as each is a blessing on their own. "Your father was always up to devilment, but I knew he had a heart as big as himself."

Mary and Joseph Kiely's headstone

Before we left Ireland we paid our respects to those resting peacefully in the big graveyard called Dean's Grange. I often wondered how my Father managed to find his Da, who is buried with Peter whom they called Padder. In the ancient section of this giant bone yard he pointed out his grandparent's headstone. He said, 'I'd only been in Canada a year when my Granddad had the accident. Pat said that witness statements read that Bubbles had bolted. Maybe a car horn tooted and frightened her? Anyway, Granddad stood up to rein her in, but he was knocked out of the trap by the limb of a tree, and pronounced dead at the scene, May 22, 1959. I was glad he didn't suffer, but it broke my heart not to be there to pay my respects to the man. I loved him."

Back at school I wrote a story about my trip to Ireland and read it in front of Father Culnan, an old nun, and a young nun. They all wore black and white habits, but the nuns had long rosary beads around their waists. The funny man, Father Culnan, was a regular visitor to our class. I was welcomed back by my friends Ramona, Laura-lee, Wendy, and Laura. My very best friend at St. Pat's was Francis MacGregor, and my very best friend in the world was Wanda James.

Wanda and I had a crush on Davy Jones from the hit TV show, "The Monkees". We would never miss the mad cap adventures of Peter Tork, Mike Nesbitt, Mickey Dolense, and Davy Jones. "*Here we come . . . walkin' down the street . . . we get the funniest looks from everyone we meet*". We'd kiss the album cover and giggle and talk to Davy like he was in the room. We screamed and freaked out when she got tickets to their show at the CNE on August 25, 1969, for her birthday. We were two of the thousands of girls too young to appreciate the opening act, Jimi Hendrix. I totally remember asking, "Who's the black guy? That's not Davy Jones." I screamed and Wanda fainted when our heart throb took the stage.

Mr. James had the honour of driving John Lennon, Yoko Ono, and some of their entourage to Niagara Falls in the late sixties. Lennon had been banned from the States at the time. He was considered a high profile peace activist. Everything had to be kept top secret, hush-hush. Mr. James thought he'd play a trick on his wife by having someone from the Limo Company call her and say that they had all been arrested by Customs at the border. Mrs. James didn't think this funny at all. She said, "Al came home with his tail between his legs, and a black and white peace-sign-button souvenir from John Lennon." He said, "They were with a big group, and his son, Julian, was with them."

Chapter Five

The Big Picture and the Four Families

I always accepted and embraced the fact that I am part of this big circle. My extended family simply goes on and on and on. My Mother takes things as they come. She says, "Let the circle be".

The French Connection made a point to stay in touch and be together monthly at the very least. Cars filled driveways and parked in rows on the street when there was a family gathering. Occasionally we would go to St. Catherine's and visit the Dionne's and their five kids, or to Fort Erie to see Uncle Paul's gang or John Beaulieu, Aunt Freda, and their boys. More regularly we had visits with the four families that lived within a one-hour-drive: the George Beaulieu family, the Oscar Beaulieu family, the Tripp bunch, and the Kiely clan.

During summers I would spend weeks with my cousins', and they in turn would come and stay at our house. I remember piles of coats and shoes in doorways, and warm hugs and kisses from all my Aunts and Uncles. When I stayed at Denise's, she, Ginette, and I would go to the indoor pool at Pape Avenue. In the summer we might go to the outdoor Olympic Pool at 'The Beaches'. We had so much fun as kids sitting around a table and eating meals together. When I stayed at Jeannette's we went shopping, and to movies at Yorkdale Mall. There was always a table of parents, and a table or two of kids, and it was always pot-luck and plenty. Everyone was always welcome, but it was expensive to travel so we didn't get to see the ones in St. Kit's or Fort Erie as often. Whenever we did, the warm feeling was always the same. We were all from the same tribe.

One of the best memories was the summers of 1968 and 1969 when the four families went camping for a week at Bon Echo Provincial Park. It was Uncle Ross's idea. The Tripp family were avid campers. Auntie Agnes always wore a kerchief and bikini. She had a knack for turning a compliment into an insult, and then playing dumb about it. She would say something like, "Your eyebrows are too thin, or maybe it is your nose that is too big." The funny part of it was she was always saying, "Ross says this, and Ross says that. Ross wouldn't do this, and Ross wouldn't do that!" I had to wonder who was talking. I was big, and got numerous little friendly reminders of this as I buttered my toast. Although his wife was easy on the eyes, she could be painful on the ears; so I used to feel sorry for my Uncle Ross, having to listen to the nasal nagger. He was my best Uncle Ross.

He had a red and white boat with a 55 Chrysler motor. During the afternoons Uncle Ross took everyone for water-ski rides. Sometimes I rode in the boat as the observer, and my job was to tell him if the skier fell, or tapped their heads which meant to go home. Sometimes he drove his boat in circles creating a whip effect and monster waves. If the skier didn't wipe out because they were spinning too fast, he would run his boat straight through the giant waves. It was a guy thing.

It was just a matter of time before the person on the end of the rope would shout, "Hit it!" to indicate they were ready, and the throttle lever went down. When I was four and five years old I had ridden on the front of my Father's skis at Uncle Gill's lake. At eight it was time for me to learn to ski by myself.

Auntie Agnes was my in-water coach; she held my legs together and positioned me with the rope between my skis. I was ready. I finally got to yell "Hit it!" After six or seven "Hit it's", and then up, up, up, splat . . . or glug, glug, glug, we had to give up. I was a lost cause, and other people were waiting for their turns. I was waterlogged and pissed off anyway. Uncle Ross, out of kindness, said, "Maybe next time, Paul?" I replied, "Ya, maybe, if you'd learn how to drive a boat." and I stomped down the beach while the adults chuckled at the spoiled brat. My Mother admitted I was spoiled, but insisted I wasn't rotten to the core.

Auntie Agnes was famous for her dandelion wine and choke-cherry jelly. She loved eccentric hats, rummage sales, and church bazaars. She was skinny, and hyper, and played solitaire for hours while her kids did the chores.

Uncle Oscar was a postman, and his wife, Aunt Lise, was somebody important at Toronto Dominion Bank. He had fought in the Korean War, and my Mother doesn't know what happened over there but her brother sure returned afraid of snakes. He used to fix radios in Montreal before they moved to Coxwell Avenue near Danforth in 1958. I only remember Uncle Oscar with salty hair. He was a Scout Leader and a good father to the twins, Denise and Denis, who were a couple of years older than me, and little Ginette who was my age but half my size. Ginette seemed younger, and she preferred to play with Colleen and Suzanne.

Uncle George and Aunt Bernice had Chris, Jeannette, Marcel, and Suzanne; and because he worked out of town for a big roofing company, his family time was very precious. He was a burly Frenchman with dark wavy hair, a deep warm laugh, and sincere green eyes. He hugged like a teddy bear, and was furry like one too. He would toss his boys around in the water. We all loved Uncle George or "Brother George" as my Mother called him.

Aunt Bernice was the first adult that we kids would get taller than, because she finished growing at four feet, ten inches tall. She made the best shortbread cookies at Christmas time. Her brown eyes sparkled, and she had tiny hands and feet like a doll. Chris and Jeannette were already taller than their mother, but if she wanted Chris's attention she'd just pull him down to her eye level by his ear.

My Dad was generally 'making hay' in the summer time, so he only camped on weekends. He was a rough and ready camper, so we had to borrow a lot of gear from the Tripp's. My Mom was brave staying with them because I was a handful, Colleen a toddler, and Sean still a baby. My Mother got four new front teeth after Sean was born, and she smiled and talked more now. I didn't mind her old ones, but she did. Colleen had fly-a-way hair, and she usually had a runny nose. She was completely absorbed by the zipper on the tent. Zipper up, and out crawls Colleen all smiles; zipper down, zipper up and she's back in the tent, zipper down. She'd be covered in dust and dirt from crawling around and in and out; so we'd head down to the beach where the sand was hot and dip her in the cool water to clean her off. I thought my bare feet were the most marvellous thing, toes sifting through the sand. They could run, jump, swim, dance; they took me everywhere. Once Colleen was washed, my Mother would prop her in the sand. She had a white sun-hat with a chin strap to protect her little head from the sun - her little head with a dime-sized bald birthmark on the crown. It wasn't long before Colleen's bright eyes would take long blinks, and she would weave and bob from the lulling sound of the waves rolling onto shore. My Mother would pick up her little one, coddle her in a blanket, and lay her down in the shade.

Jeannette and Denise were boy crazy and Gail and I were horse crazy, but when it came to playing mermaids we were all crazy. Gail usually got cold first. I was always the youngest in my gang of cousins, and my parents were the youngest in the gang of adults. We needed these people, our extended family. My Mother could always ask her sister, or sisters-in-law, for help or advice; and the men were the same because Uncle George said, "We're all in this boat together." I felt safe and respected as a kid, and in turn respected the parents. If Aunts Lise or Bernice asked me to fetch something, I just did. I usually rolled my eyes for effect when Auntie Agnes made a request, but it was just part of the act. I would always oblige.

We'd go off all day on adventures. Denise and Gail were eleven and Jeannette was ten. We spied on the Park Rangers, or on people going in and out of the outhouses. We would scrounge around empty campsites, and one time we found a can of brown beans intact. Denise banged it on a rock until it split open, and we took turns sucking the guts out of the can. Patsy was about sixteen and very pretty. She had her mother's looks and won a beauty contest in her hometown of Richmond Hill. She motioned us over to meet this guy she was sitting with at a picnic table. He had long hair and a well worn denim jacket with a smiley-face patch on it. He said he had been in the Vietnam War, and proved it by letting us feel a bullet that had travelled down his arm and was lodged in the end of his thumb. I'll never forget the perfect shape of that bullet under the skin. He said he was here to get away from it all.

Patsy and the bullet guy took us up a dangerous path on the flat front of a rock face. At the top the view was fantastic and the blueberries were giants. We sat and plucked and ate. Patsy slipped on the way down and sanded some skin off her ass; but she was alright. We were sworn to secrecy. There were rusty red hand prints on the rock face at Bon Echo that I just knew were the real deal: maybe the worn old warpaint hands of Tecumseh, or perhaps some other brave warrior? From a young age I was fascinated and humbled by the harmony with nature and sur-vival techniques of the Native Canadians. I was deeply moved by a commercial on television where Chief Dan George had a tear running down his cheek while standing in a garbage dump. In the sixties we learned about pollution and how the industrial revolution was poisoning our planet.

I could go to anyone of my Aunts or Uncles for anything, especially the Tripps, because they'd packed everything, even their big black and white Springer Spaniel called Waggs. She was a dear dog that watched Uncle Ross, and waited near shore hunting for minnows. We shared a common clothes line tied between two trees where everybody's towels or bathing suits were strung and hung. When it rained we waited it out under tarps. Rainwater pooled in the low spots, and the men would push up the low spot and the water would run off like a waterfall. The sandy earth covered in dry pine needles drank up the water, and in no time it was as if it had never rained at all. I may have been spoiled, almost rotten even, but I was lucky and I knew it.

The adults played cards, and we'd play Chinese checkers or Snakes and Ladders in tents during mosquito hour; and when the buzzing of the blood-thirsty bugs decreased, we'd emerge. When we were catching fireflies in jars, I heard the distinct sound of a loon's call from somewhere on the lake.

The campfire snapped and popped, and sparks flew out of it. The night was warm so we all sat or stood at least two feet back from the red coals and yellow flames. Various people gathered around, some with marshmallows on sticks turning gold, or in Marcel's case, burnt black because he liked his that way. I know Auntie Agnes was there because I still flinch at the memory of her voice screeching "Ross!" above the hum of the others. It happened so fast, so unexpectedly. In hindsight doesn't it always? There we were, most of us anyways, just toasting marshmallows around a camp fire surrounded by tall pines. If your eyes followed the trail of smoke up, there was a blue-black sky bedazzled by stars. I believe Jeannette, Denise, Gail and I had just finished singing our song:

> *"Here comes Granny,*
> *swinging on the outhouse door*
> *without her night-tee.*
> *Waiting for the garbage man,*
> *who was a playboy.*
> *Could you ever ask for more?*
> *Two dollars please!"*

Before Uncle George got up for more wood, he stoked the fire. He and Auntie Agnes took turns with the poker. Yep, that's when it happened alright. Uncle George, the guy my Father insisted was 99.9% saint, my Uncle George that wore a Labatt's 50 beer-can hat and thoroughly enjoyed an Old Port cigar. This same Uncle George who was Aunt Bernice's afternoon delight raised the axe that fell off its handle and came down right on top of his head. The axe bounced off his skull and hit the ground. Uncle George fell to his knees, blood trickling down his forehead; then his eyes rolled back and Uncle Oscar caught him. Aunt Bernice was at his side. Auntie Agnes and my Mother suggested we kids say a prayer, so we did, the Our Father. Uncle George was talking and they helped him to a chair. Aunt Lise got an ice pack. My Father held up Uncle Ross's flashlight so Aunt Bernice and all other sets of eyes could inspect the gash. We overheard Uncle Oscar say, "A clean cut, right on the top of his head."

Then I heard Uncle George say, "That ice feels good," and I saw him smirk before he had another swig of his beer. They'd all had a few pops. Where was the hospital around here anyway?

When camping, there always seemed to be that one mosquito that buzzed around my head and kept me awake, so it wasn't unusual to sleep deep down in the sleeping bag. In the morning Uncle George had a headache. He showed us his goose egg in the daylight, and we were invited to touch it if we wanted to, but I didn't.

Chapter Six

Why? That's Why!

My old man had a big presence. He said his bellowing baritone voice was an Irish whisper. He wholeheartedly believed one could move mountains with prayers, and that anything was possible. He had a no-bullshit rule; wouldn't hand it out, and wouldn't take it in return. We went to church, feared God, recited the Rosary and Ten Commandments, and mostly ate fish on Fridays. Sunday was the day of rest. It was family day. We'd get up and scramble to get washed and dressed in time for nine o'clock Mass. If we missed it, no bother; there was another service at eleven. It just meant brunch would be lunch because it was a sin to eat before receiving Holy Communion. "They" made exceptions for the elderly, small children, and pregnant women, whoever "they" were.

The Kielys were famous for getting to church just in the nick of time. We'd just find seats, and no sooner sit our arses down than we would have to stand for the procession. Most Sundays we simply followed the priest in. I loved the way the sun shone through the stained glass and the congregation joining in on the old familiar hymns like Amazing Grace or How Great Thou Art. Even though the priest said and did pretty much the same routine every week, I hardly understood any of it. I soon tuned out and had my own conversations with God. I thanked the Creator for my very existence and my family; and I distinctly remember asking, "God, what were you thinking? My parents are like two sticks of dynamite, and I'm their mixed-up kid!"

My Mother used to say, "Half Irish and half French-Canadian. This makes you Holy Smoke." There I'd be, going through the motions, tuned out, but dialled in enough to sit, and stand, and kneel.

My parents asked for my opinions, and they shared their fears and showed their emotions. I was taught to replace fear with faith, and to have faith in God's plan. I knew to sit quietly for an hour in God's house because if I did there would be a treat after.

There were images of angels and archangels stepping on the necks of serpents and demons, but Jesus was all about compassion and forgiveness. He never stood on any necks, but was brutally crucified and hung on a cross behind the altar. Jesus healed the sick, walked on water, and spoke in parables using real life experiences as examples for His teachings. It is from life's lessons we gain our greatest knowledge. Some priests, on the other hand, appeared to have little or no compassion or forgiveness. There were regular sermons on guilt and fear; and how even if you did your very best, it still wouldn't be good enough. My Mother said, "You're dammed if you do, and you're dammed if you don't."

We dipped our fingers in the Holy Water font and made the sign of the cross before leaving. The congregation milled around smiling and shaking hands. Orderly traffic exited the parking lot and now the day was ours. Dad said, "We're washed, dressed, and blessed, and ready to seize the day."

He also said, "All we can do is try, and try again to be our best like the good guy, Jesus. We must fight against the lures of evil and selfishness, and follow the golden rule which is to love one another as I have loved you."

When I asked him if I could go to a party or sleep over at a friend's, he generally said "No"; and if I questioned "Why," he'd say "That's why!" My friends were always welcome at our place, my Father said, "I get a peaceful sleep when I know where you are." Dad generally said "No" and Mom usually said "Yes". When she asked him why he always said "No." he told her, "I'm buying time to think. I can change a no to a yes, but I can't change a yes to a no."

I might have been eight when the teatime story was about the girl who disobeyed her mother. My Father said, "There was this lovely young girl in Dublin who wanted to go to a dance, but her mother said she was too young for dances. So this girl lied to her mother and said she was going to visit a sick friend and she went to this dance anyway. There she met a young man, a handsome young man, and they laughed and danced the night away. At the end of the evening when the young man was helping the girl on with her coat, she glanced down, and where his feet should be she saw the hooves of a goat."

"When she turned around, her handsome young man had transformed into Satan himself. The young girl had spent the night dancing with the devil. She was never right after that, and that's why you must always be a good girl and do as you're told."

I remember lying in bed looking at the sliver of light under the door. I wouldn't move for fear of the devil that I imagined waiting for me under my bed. Dad said, "In the graveyard in the old country there was this boy that hit his mother, and when he died his hand stuck out his grave. There was another fella that kicked his old man in the backside; when he died, his arse cheeks stuck out of the ground, and people passing by took them for a bike stand." Honestly, God, what were you thinking?

Chapter Seven

The Horse Bug

U ncle Oscar and Aunt Lise were considering buying a one-acre plot of land in Ballantrae, and our family was invited to see the property as my Father would be building them a new house. When we arrived I wasn't impressed. It was an overgrown flat narrow acre between two houses. The day was hot, the top was down on our car, and Mom chose to sun herself in the passenger seat and mind Sean when we stopped at a store for a cold drink.

In 1969, where Aurora Sideroad crosses Highway 48, Ogden's Garage was on the south-east corner, a hotel restaurant on the south-west corner, and this old store on the north-east corner. We ended up going up the steps of the Ballantrae General Store. There was a funky smell to the place. The chubby person behind the counter had short cropped grey hair, and was outfitted in green "Dickie" brand work pants and shirt that were separated by a thick black belt. On the feet, black safety boots. I was confused because this person had big boobs, and when my Dad spoke, a female voice replied.

Pixie had followed Colleen into the store, and we were having a look around while Dad got three bottles of 7-Up to share out of the fridge. There was a lot of hardware, like pulleys and washers and things; and it got dimmer towards the back because the only light was provided by the big front window. The floors were wide pine planks with paths worn into them. None of us had noticed but the shopkeeper did and shouted, "Git that male the hell outta here!" When we looked, Pixie had his hind leg up, and he was squirting on a case of pop.

Colleen Kiely and Pixie

Colleen said, "What's yer problem? This is only a stinky store anyway! Come on, Pixie." And they trotted outside.

On our way down the steps, I asked, "Dad, was that a man or a woman?"

He said, "Pauline, that's what you call a Shim. Not sure if she's a she or a him."

Uncle Oscar and Aunt Lise changed their minds about the lot. They decided to buy a cottage on an island. So my Father bought the lot. Apparently there were nine lots for sale between two three-acre properties. When Dad was building our house, he was also building one down the road for Jan Vanderson who said "Jan is like John in Holland."

We still lived in the house in Markham on May 6, 1970. I remember my Dad answered the phone, and called my Mom from the other room. She was standing in the kitchen and had only said "Hello" before crumpling to the ground like a limp rag doll and crying into her hands.

Alice Beaulieu - 1967

Dad looked at me and in a soft voice said, "That's Uncle Oscar. Memère has passed away." She had been staying with Paul, and they were just watching Dialing for Dollars on television when she took three deep breaths.

Paul said, "A peace came over the room, and I knew she was gone, just like that."

*Yolande Kiely,
her sisters and nieces*

The Beaulieu Brothers

What consoled the family was the fact that their Mother never suffered and that she departed so gracefully. They had all been together just two weeks ago celebrating the marriage of her youngest son, Gabriel, to Olga. Gabe was the last one to get married.

Shortly afterwards, our family's belongings were moved in pick-up trucks by family and friends from 49 Sherwood Forest Drive to that one-acre lot on the Aurora Sideroad in Ballantrae. I was ten, and remember being more than a little confused and annoyed by the relocation. I liked Markham, and I missed my friends. No more shopping at the plaza or going to the matinee. I was the eldest of three children; and when my Grade Four year ended at St. Pat's, I braced myself for what I was certain would be my worst summer ever.

My Father, being the builder, moved us into a construction site. Our framed bungalow wrapped in Domtar was barely a shelter: it did offer a bathtub, flush toilet, a couple of pigtail light bulbs, and two electrical outlets, but there were no walls or closets or anything. My Mom was such a good sport, hanging floral curtains around the bathroom's framed-in two by fours. For the last few weeks of school Mom drove us back and forth to St. Patrick's in Markham to finish the year. She was behind the wheel of a red Ford Galaxy 500 rag-top with white leather interior. Colleen loved the song *Jeremiah Was a Bullfrog*, by Three Dog Night. All ears were tuned to 1050 Chum. She was "Coll McCool." Sean wasn't in school yet. He would curl up on the floor like a kitten and sleep. Pixie never missed a road trip. He loved to have his face in the wind and dance back and forth across the backseat.

Our neighbours to the left were three old brothers we called "the Gruff's" because they were grumpy. They never came outside much; and when they did, it was to complain about dust, noise, or kids. On the other side were the Wedleys, Jack and Becky, and their two girls, Joanne and Jackie. The Wedleys were recent transplants from a posh neighbourhood in Unionville, or as they called it, "Onionville." Mr. Wedley was a salesman for

Seagrams VO Whiskey. They had cases and cases of booze bottles in their basement. White-haired Jack Wedley was a retired football player who had had a couple of good seasons with the Argonauts.

On Saturday mornings my Da sang;

> *"If I had a hammer,*
> *I'd hammer in the morning,*
> *I'd hammer in the evening, all over this land.*
> *I'd hammer out a rainbow,*
> *I'd hammer out a warning.*
> *I'd hammer out the love between*
> *my brothers and my sisters, all over this land."*

He banged and sawed, and caulked and taped; and usually in the afternoons some warm body would drop by to check on progress, or lend a hand. Mom was the perfect hostess with her Dagwood sandwiches and pots of coffee. Dad said, "Work is serious but doesn't have to be miserable. If you enjoy what you doing and see positive results, what more can you ask for? Life isn't a bed of roses. Life is what you make it, kid!"

For a young man my old man knew exactly what he was doing. He seemed to have endless energy. He was a workhorse now. The bricklayers would sing "Arrivederchi Roma" and "O Sole Mio" all day long. They let me "mix-a-the-mortar" and "lay-a-the-bricks".

Colleen and I shared a bed, and one morning when our sleepy eyes opened, there were a pair of crows like a live version of the cartoon characters *Heckle and Jeckle* perched on our dresser. Their curious heads turned this way and that so their beady black eyes could get a better look at us. When we screamed, they flew up and out the hole in the roof where the fireplace chimney would someday be.

"Mom, there's gotta be someone you can phone. Really, Mom, Dad has gone crazy." I said.

She was no comfort, "He hasn't gone crazy, Pauline. He's Irish, and this is just a bit of his gypsy spirit."

So I rolled my eyes and went for a walk.

This bug is invisible, and how it strikes, a mystery; but it's an incurable disease that I'm utterly delighted to have contracted. Nothing but tall grasses mixed with wild flowers and various insects. I told my troubles to the butterflies. The sun scorched and the cicada sang as my feet carried me over the crest of a hill, and there they were. Three Palomino horses. I had never seen real horses up close and, to date, only ridden the ten cent pony at the Dominion grocery store. When I got closer, these majestic animals met me at the fence, their tails swishing and heads nodding. The little one looked me right in the eye, and breathless I stared back. Their pasture had been nipped down tight, so I pulled grass from the field and fed them for who knows how long.

In the distance I heard a commotion towards the back of the property: whistlin', hootin', and hollerin'. I snuck up for a closer look. There was a sandy-haired boy, with no shirt or shoes, galloping on a big brown horse. His dog was running circles around him and barking like he was talking to him. There was a small herd of horses in this field, and the boy and his dog appeared to be chasing them.

His horse stopped suddenly and froze, looking in my direction. I'd been spotted, and this boy made a clucking sound and motioned his horse my way.

"Who's there? Are you spying on me?" he asked.

"No," I said, "I was just feeding these horses and then I heard you."

"Do you like horses?

"I guess so."

"Get up on the fence and then hop on behind me. This is Mandy and I'm Bryan, Bryan Cauldin."

Before I knew it, I was on a horse. We giggled and bounced trotting. Bryan told me about his ranch, and then he introduced me to his best friend, the black Lab he called Luke.

My parents spent their summer consumed with finishing the house, and I spent the afternoons feeding Palominos and riding Mandy with Bryan. I thought things were going well until one afternoon when his buddies came around. The boys coaxed me up a tree and then proceeded to tie me up in it with binder twine. "It's not your fault; you're a girl." Bryan shouted before leaving me there. My Mother sent Colleen to find me, and she did; but Mom had to come herself and climb the tree to cut me loose.

Bryan came to our house on his horse to apologize. When I was introducing my new friend to my Father, he said, "Hey, Bryan, pull this finger!" So he did, and my Dad backfired. I blushed, and Bryan laughed hysterically.

I started Grade Five at Ballantrae Public School that September. I was in an all-girl class of thirty-one, and Mrs. Weldon was our teacher. I was the new kid. It was a dismal October evening when I lined up three of Father's saw-horses in our newly built detached garage. They hadn't just finished the house that summer, but built a garage too. I was chatting away to my pretend horses, and my body bucked when my Da cleared his throat.

"Who are you talking to?" he asked.

I replied, "My horse."

"Your what? Never mind, it's time for your dinner," he said.

I watched him scratching his noggin when I followed him to the house.

My Mother referred to my Father as 'the Lord and Master'. He was the boss. She would say, "He's the King, and I'm the Queen. He messes and I clean." During tea 'the Lord and Master' announced, "Pauline and I are going out on Saturday to see if we can find her a horse. I'll have no child of mine talking to herself."

My Mother said nothing, but stood up and walked over to the closet, opened the doors, and started talking.

He said, "Who are you talking to?"

She said, "My fur coat!"

Dad's hat was red, his truck was red, and his neck was red, but he said we were greenhorns! We went to the Co-Op Feed Store in Stouffville inquiring where to buy a horse. The man behind the counter gave Dad directions and said, "Get over and see Dan Barkey. He'll fix you up."

When we got to Barkey's, there was a hand-painted sign that read "Horses, bought and sold." My heart was pounding as fast as Dad's knuckles on the door. A lady answered, Mrs. Barkey, and it seems we'd just missed Danny, who was out for the day. While my Father was talking to this woman, explaining where we lived and answering questions like how old I was, and what was our price range, I went over to a paddock with four horses in it. They were just standing about looking jaded. There was a black one near enough to the fence so I jumped on. I could see Mrs. Barkey smiling in the doorway, and then my Father turned to see what she was looking at. "Jesus, Pauline, get down out of that. Jainey, that child." He was always saying, 'Jainey, that child'. "Is that horse for sale, Mrs. Barkey?"

"They're all for sale, Mr. Kiely, I'll have Danny give you a call."

It was a long day in earshot of the phone, but finally it rang. Dad said, "Barkey will be coming by tomorrow, Pauline; so you and I have our work cut out for us."

It was cold and damp and the chill had got into my bones. My hands and feet were so cold while I held those fence rails for the little corral the two of us built outside his new garage. My Dad sunk the fence posts, and he banged together a stall. I just held the ends of boards and his level once in a while. Mostly I kept him company.

At the end of the following day, a pick-up truck with a horse's head hanging over a plywood box turned into our driveway. There was a cloud of dust when the truck stopped. The driver jumped out. He hadn't reached thirty. He had dark curly hair and stunning big blue eyes. "Danny Barkey, fit as a fiddle, and at your service. I hear someone's looking for a horse." He extended his hand to my Da who shook it firmly. Dan Barkey placed a ramp up to the open tailgate, and then he backed the black horse off the truck. This horse seemed larger and more spirited; her nostrils were flared, and she was wildly calling, whinnying. Barkey passed the lead shank over to my Da.

"Try her for a month," he said. "The bridle and halter are part and parcel. I'll give youse the loan of a saddle while youse get acquainted; and if you're not happy you'll get a full refund in thirty days. I'm a phone call away."

"That's fair enough," my Father said, while scribbling his autograph on a cheque.

"What's her name?" I asked.

Barkey said, "You can call her what you like, but I'd call that mare, Jet, cause she's Jet-black. Her teeth tell me she's about seven, and I'd bet there's maybe a bit of Morgan blood in that mare." Barkey's country twang was new to me. With a wink and his paper money in his pocket, he was gone.

Pauline Kiely and Jet - 1971

Even though I pulled on the reins with all my might, this crazy Jet had no brakes. Those first few days and weeks I fell off a lot more than I stayed on. Sometimes we'd get going along nicely, and then she'd turn sharply and off I'd go. I mostly rode bareback because the saddle was so heavy. I called these sharp turns when I flew off and got the wind knocked out of me 'Sharpies'. Once I was breathing again, I caught her and climbed aboard from the nearest fence. This was my horse and I was going to ride it. I sought some advice from expert horseman Bryan Cauldin. He came over with Mandy and after the horses touched noses and stomped the ground, they appeared to be friends. Jet would follow Mandy. Bryan said I needed a curb chain to slow her down, recommended a helmet; and he had a little first-aid kit of gauze and bandages for my scrapes when we went riding.

I rode my horse everyday for hours, round and round in circles, one way, and then the other to let her know that when I asked her to turn, she should turn; and when I asked her to whoa, she should stop. Jet and I were inseparable. I rode her to a vacant field across the road from Ballantrae Public School where she grazed while I was in class. At the end of the day I'd canter up the side of the road, amusing the passengers of school buses that passed.

Bryan called on me early summer mornings. He and I would go on adventures taking trails and some roads or ditches to Island Lake where we could go swimming on our horses. He had gotten a new horse, a pinto he named Comanchie. Comanchie was really, really fast. He was a gelding with a pie-ball, that's a blue and brown eye. Bryan's sisters took turns riding Mandy.

In the water, riding Jet was like riding a merry-go-round. She splashed before submerging and actually swimming. I would just hold on loosely to her mane and grip with my legs. Jet even put her nose underwater and snorted like a hippo. After the swim she would stand calm chest deep in the water and she would let kids climb up and dive off her back. Once some poops popped up in the water, and some kid dove into it. That kid's parents made a big fuss; so I had to keep the horse out of the water if parents were around.

On a Saturday at the Stouffville Sales Barn, vendors sold everything from baby ducks to diamonds. There were goats and bunnies, and it was a real carnival atmosphere for bargain hunters. Dad told us we were on the prowl for a 'wing-wong-for-a-whooser'.

I remember being there this one hot Saturday afternoon. Colleen, Sean, and I were strolling along the aisles and stalls in our parents' wake. Someone said they were hungry, and Dad bought this big salami after having a sample from a meat vendor. He peeled back the wax paper, bit this salami, and passed it to my Mother. She had a bite and passed it to me. In turn I passed it onto Colleen who passed it on to Sean, and back to snickering Dad.

On the way home from the Sales Barn I was pestering Colleen and Sean in the back seat, putting my hand on them, just winding them up. Colleen started whining, and suddenly Father's great arm and club of a hand hurled across the back seat, giving me a swat.

"Stop that, you tyrant." he said.

My Mother said, "Three brats and another one on the way."

I was speechless. I had become friends with Bryan's older sister Amy who was fourteen, slender, and dainty. She was very fussy about her appearance, but she wore a t-shirt with a picture of *Uncle Sam* and the caption *Mr. Dirt Wants You!* The next time I saw Amy I said, "I think my Mom is having a baby."

"She is. She told my Mom two weeks ago." Amy said.

Over the winter my Mother's belly grew, and by Easter she was calling herself a Buddha. Sean would sit on her lap and drive his dinky-cars over her belly, and he would make a noise like a car engine sound. He seemed so contented that Mom was having this baby. "I need a brother 'cause my sisters drive me crazy."

That Spring a bunch of us at school had taken to racing garter snakes at recess. We kept our racers in shoe boxes on a bed of grass. I came home with my snake on May 1st, 1971, and wanted my Mother's attention, but she was on the phone. She wouldn't get off the phone. She had her back to me, and I wanted to show her my snake. So I lowered it over her head in front of her face. She yelled, "Go next door and get Mrs. Wedley."

I was ten. I put the snake back in the box and did what I was told. I knocked on Wedley's door and said, "Mrs. Wedley, can you come to our house? My Mom needs you." Mrs. Wedley followed me through the bushes and split-rail cedar fence, and my Mother appeared so relieved. "Becky, my water's broke and I can't find John. Can you drive me to the hospital?"

Mrs. Wedley, who had been a nurse, immediately took charge. I took Colleen and Sean next door to be minded by Joanne, and Jackie and I waited at our house for my Father. Mrs. Wedley grabbed her purse and keys and drove my Mother to Scarborough Centenary Hospital.

It was dusk and had become very foggy by the time his truck's headlights came down the driveway. When he came in, Jackie said, "Hello, Mr. Kiely," and then, "I'm going to go home to do my chores now."

"Where's your Mother? What the hell is going on?" he asked.

"She has gone to the hospital with Mrs. Wedley." I answered.

"Holy shit, I think I'm a dead man. She said this morning that she thought today might be the day. Put your horse in and we'll go and see her."

So I went out to put Jet in but it had become even denser fog. When I went to bring her through the door of the garage, she spooked. Jet jerked my arm, got away on me, and ran off. I could hear her but I couldn't see my black horse in this fog. I shook a bucket of oats, which usually got her attention, but not this time. I found out that in spring it isn't this kind of oats that a horse wants. I went inside and asked Dad for some help. With the two of us chasing her, we finally caught 'the bitch in heat!' an hour later. It took his man-muscle to lead her steaming nostrils home and into her stall.

Dad said, "Jaysus, would you look at the time! Your Mother's going to have my head."

"And mine," I said, "I didn't know she was having the baby, and scared her with my snake."

"Well, we'll face the music together then," he said.

The limited visibility made the trip to Scarborough even longer, and when we arrived at the maternity ward, the nurse at reception said, "Visiting hours are long over, Mr. Kiely." He was helplessly trying to explain our circumstances when my Mother came walking softly down the hall. The three of us sat together in a lounge.

Dad said, "Lovey, I am the King of all Arse-holes. What a feckin' day, and then to top it off that bloody horse taking off . . . I am so sorry."

Mom said, "Lovey, he's a beautiful baby boy. He's a great little man."

His eyes filled with tears, and they hugged and a quick kiss, and he said, "You're a great little woman, Yolande. What will we call him?"

And I suggested, "Jim, how about Jim?"

Dad said, "Does he look like a Jim?"

Mom said, "He even smells like a Jim."

Dad said, "I'll tell you what we'll do. We'll call him Jim, but on his birth certificate we'll put the name James, after the Granddad's brother."

I was pushing eleven when Jim was born. I loved showing him off to my friends. Dad told me this gob of goo on the baby's belly button was a bumble bee that would fly away in a few days. Colleen, Sean, and I had watched this movie called, "The Scarlet Pimpernel," starring Danny Kaye. It was set in Old England and they were looking for the infant prince whom they would know by the birthmark of a blue pimpernel flower on the cheek of his butt. After that I drew all sorts of things on Jim's butt! On a Sunday night my parents often cuddled on the chesterfield while watching Goldie Hawn on *Rowan and Martin's Laugh-in*. Dad called our television 'the juke box' and he scared us by saying that if we watched it too much, our eyes would go square.

In the winter months I hauled buckets of water from the sink in the basement of the house to the barn for Jet. I had to keep bringing them until she had her fill. Some mornings my horse would place her snout and lips on top of the water and in-hale five pails in a row; other days she wasn't thirsty, and I was stuck thawing a bucket of ice at the end of the day. I read about horses, and learned why they needed salt blocks to lick, and some grain plus good hay during the winter. I knew to de-worm my horse spring and fall. I was mucking a stall now and I wasn't talking to myself anymore.

Chapter Eight

Frog Island

The cottage located on the small island in Belmont Lake that Uncle Oscar and Aunt Lise purchased proved to be a big success in those psychedelic seventies. It took an hour and a half to get there whether we went for a Sunday-drive or stayed for a week.

The family called it 'Oscar's Island', but the popular lily pad soon became known locally as 'the little island with all the people on it' or simply 'Frog Island'. I used to think it was because of the cute little frog that his youngest, Ginette, hand-painted on the front of Uncle Oscar's fishing boat.

We were safe on our own island. Surrounded by water we were cut off from the rest of the world. You might imagine you'd have to think twice about just showing up, or what would you do if you missed your arranged ride? Would you be out of luck? Nope, this wasn't a problem on 'Frog Island' because some warm body was always hanging around at the Belmont Marina for more fuel, ice, supplies, or maybe for mechanical service by Jumpin' Jim. His daughter, Jasmine, had a beautiful voice and sang *One Tin Soldier* as she pumped the petrol. If there wasn't a familiar face around the marina, someone would be along shortly. Patsy, Chris, Denise, and Denis could all drive their parents' boats, and they did a lot.

Jumping off the dock at Frog Island - 1975

Straight out from the marina the best route is around the south tip of Big Island, and then north through a narrow between Big and Mary's Islands. Then there it is in all its glory: the 'Frog Island,' a two-bedroom log cabin with the red steel roof and cobblestone chimney. There were four, maybe five, really large pine trees, and a few smaller shrubs for vegetation, a couple of pup-tents, and a tent trailer on the east side of the cottage. Out front there was a large concrete patio with stone steps that descended to the dock where the ski boats were tied. There'd always be smoke coming from the barbeque on weekends, and generally forty-odd aunts, uncles, cousins, in-laws, out-laws, and friends, lounging around soaking up some sun. I'm not sure what the logic was but sometimes the men would pick rocks. They'd wade in the water about two or three feet from shore picking up big rocks and throwing them on shore. It was like they were trying to make the island bigger. Sometimes the men would go on strike for beer. There was also a dock on the east side of the island where the water toys were moored. Over the years we graduated from a big tire tube to a canoe, an aluminum fishing boat, and a paddle boat.

My both hands were curled tightly around the wooden bar handle of the tow rope. My knees bent, I confidently shouted, "Hit it!" to Uncle Ross before popping out of the water like an old pro now. We'd pre-arranged to circle around, so that I could drop my right ski and slalom. The water felt hard under my ski, riding the trail that the prop creates. It appeared like a road in the water. I never stayed there long because I liked to zig and zag back and forth to catch air jumping the wake of the waves. Almost everyone, every age, on 'Frog Island' went for a ski. The kids would laugh when our mothers went for a short one. Most of my cousins could get up on one ski, but not me.

The sun was warm but the spray of water was cool. My Uncle Ross was focused on what was ahead, but my spotters, Marcel and Gary, were all smiles as their hair whipped around in the boat. The three of us took turns water-skiing around Big Island. I was twelve so my body hardly complained after a twenty-minute ski. Upon return as our boat roared past the dock, dotted with spectators, I waved and let go and coasted towards them before coming to a sinking stop. My ski popped up and I took it off and pushed it ahead of me, swimming quite contented to shore.

"Was it a good one, Paul?" Uncle Ross asked.

"The best, Uncle Ross. Thanks."

Then I'd wrap up in a towel and spot for Gary with Mars, and then for Marcel with Gary. Gary and Denis were the best skiers out of the boys, and Patsy and Denise the best out of the girls. Denis would cut so extreme that his shoulder would hit the water; then he'd wipe out and skip across the surface like a stone. We all admired him, and said his Indian name would be 'Dances on Water'! Gary just kept getting better until he could ski without skis, barefoot.

In the morning we lined up with plates at Aunt Lise's famous outdoor all-you-could-eat pancake grill. After our fill of pancakes we had to stay out of the water for an hour to let our stomachs settle. While this was going on my Uncles Ross, Oscar, and George would all sort out their ropes, and when they started their engines it was time. They drove their boats all day towing us kids, on one ski, two skis, or tricky turnabout skis. Brothers George and Oscar both had Johnson 50's. Uncle Ross, being a mechanic, kept his Chrysler in top form. They weren't the best boats on the lake, but they sure weren't the worst either. We counted ourselves very lucky to have one another, and boats, at all.

We would ski double, or even triple, behind one boat. This would be hard on both skiers and the boats because both had to work harder until the boat levelled out towing the extra weight. Once we were on top of the water, this strain was relieved. I believe our record was six behind a boat, and that's only because we ran out of ski-ropes. We managed this feat by having two skiers behind each boat, but the skiers behind the center boat each held three ropes. Once all skiers were up, the boats drove alongside each other, and then the skiers passed over the ropes so that all six were eventually behind the one boat. There was no contest.

Gail had gotten a sign for the outhouse that read 4U2P. Despite how many of us there were, I don't ever remember having to wait very long. It wasn't really a place you wanted to linger anyway. The spring on the door moaned when you pulled it open, and banged when you let it go. The warm breeze carried a hint of pine, thanks to the trees' gum and drying needles on the ground.

We were all growing up together, and at sixteen Denise filled out her bikini. One day she was showing off. She put the rope handle behind her knee and she was skiing hands free. Denise was posing and put her hands behind her head and to her sides. She was acting like a stunt skier when the fastest boat on Belmont Lake, a purple sparkling *Checkmate* slowed down and cruised alongside our Johnson 50. The guys on the boat were whistling and waving at Denise who waved back, blowing them kisses thinking they were impressed by her talent. Indeed, they were impressed - by more than her talent. Her bikini top had shifted during her acrobatics. Denise hadn't noticed until Jeannette, her spotter, covered her brother Chris's eyes, and cut the engine on their boat, shouting, "Denise, look down!" Denise never ever wore that bathing suit again. She gave it to Patsy who didn't fill it out the same but never took it off.

Suzanne, Colleen, and Gail Trip - 1975

Meals were always big feeds, and potluck; nobody went hungry. There was an unwritten rule, Help Yourself. When the stars came out, there would be a fire and a few marshmallows, a bit of a sing-song; but when the mosquitoes got ravenous, the parents would congregate in the summer kitchen to light the Coleman lantern and play cards or a board game called "Whahoo."

The little ones would be tucked in for the night, but we bigger ones would flock to 'the rock' at the back of the cottage where we'd puff on glowing cigarettes. The adults knew what we were up to because when they went to relieve themselves they'd say, "Who's there?" and hear the tis, tis, tis of our precious smokes hitting the water before any reply.

When we got a little older, Gail tried smoking but she hated it. She said it was gross and that she was allergic to smoke. The rest of us ate the menthol Cameo cancer sticks we pooled our money to buy. Ridiculous, really, that as a kid I could buy anything at that little store on Belmont Lake that was basically a sign over a cottage porch converted by some shelving, a counter, and cash register that disguised itself as a store.

The lady behind the counter wore a dirty apron that she kept wiping her hands on. It was fastened at the back by a droopy bow. She had a great tan and bleached yellow hair. She didn't smile much, but she would manage to crack one when she was taking your money. We never hung around long once we got our precious tobacco, the contraband that we'd have to hide from our parents. Everyone who was considered cool smoked in those days, and I so wanted to be counted amongst the *cool*.

The gang at Frog Island on a Sunday afternoon - 1975

I think Denis heard about Deer River first. He and Chris had checked it out before Jeannette, Chris, Denise, Marcel, Gary, Ginette, Denis, and I piled in to the fishing boat and put-putted our way there. Deer River was a bit of a trailer park down river where there was a rope swing and sandy beach. There the bunch of us would go to swing a bit, and hang out. I remember singing "Smoke on the Water" while treading water with a lit butt, and thinking I had the world by the tail.

One morning Marcel put too much peanut butter on his knife. As he scraped the excess back into the jar, Auntie Agnes started, "Marcel, that is bad manners. You took that peanut butter; so you should eat that peanut butter. Why did you take so much if you didn't want so much? Can't you see? You had that on your knife, and now you put it back into the jar."

Marcel says, "Auntie Agnes, I took too much peanut butter, so I put some back in the jar. Where do you want me to wipe it, if not back into the jar? Should I wipe it on the curtains, on my leg, or wipe it on my mother? Next time I'll try to be a little more careful!"

Brenna Kiely immigrated to Canada in 1970. Initially she had stayed with Kate and Dave in Stouffville. Brenna had long dark hair now but those same bright blue eyes I'd met when I was seven. She had a tiny frame and a radiant smile, and she got standing applause whenever she sang Petulia Clarke's song *Puppet on a String*. Brenna was introduced to one of Uncle Dave's friends, a lean tanned guy with wavy dark hair and dark eyes named Dan Gildener. As it turned out, Dan was just one of those down-to-earth-sincerely-nice guys that my Dad said, "You can't help but like." Brenna didn't drive, but Dan brought her to visit. Like my Mother and Father, John and Yolande, they became Dan and Brenna in September of 1972.

Granny Kiely came with Maggie for the wedding. Maggie wore a beautiful emerald green dress. Dr. Brooks found an ulcer on Granny's leg that had swelled up between the stress of travelling, changes to her diet, and the wedding schedule; so she had to spend a lot of her stay with the 'ole legs' elevated in bed. Her legs were tired, and those red hands had seen many dishes and scalded many nappies.

I do remember her having dinner at our house as my Mother had me peel a pile of extra potatoes. Granny, when polishing off all these extra spuds, leans over to me and says, "You see that dog out there through the glass?" Of course I could see our black mutt, Tramp, on the other side of the sliding door, drooling and slobbering; so I answered, "Yes." And says she, "He's one fella that will be glad to see the back of me."

One night Uncle Ross and Auntie Agnes came over with his dad, Len Tripp. He and Granny reminisced about days gone by, wartimes. She was giggling and lit up, enjoying the company. In some of my future letters I would tease that her boyfriend was asking for her. I was able to introduce some of my friends to my Irish Granny.

My Mother took her for a ride to Bristol Ponds to show her the fine houses her 'genius son', as she was calling him, had built and was building. My Father's clients opened their homes to my Granny, and she saw things she said "to the likes I've never imagined".

Bristol Ponds was a custom home development. My Father had won the contract to be the main contractor for the developer of these luxury estates on one and two acre lots. These estates had cedar closets for the wife's fur coats, and two-story libraries with wrought iron ladders that travel along oak bookshelves. There were saunas and in-door pools, wall safes, and the kitchens were state-of-the-art. The Perry's, the Harper's, the Phillip's, and others were full of praises.

Dad got the bulk of his supplies from Schell Lumber in Stouffville. He said, "There are two banks in Stouffville, The Credit Union, and Schell Lumber." When Percy Schell offered him a new set of screw drivers for Christmas one year, my Father said, "Percy, we've been doing business for a few years now. You must have made a mistake. I can't drink those!"

All the boys behind the counter laughed and Percy said, "We know, Kiely. You're an Irishman." Then he pulled out a forty ounce bottle of *Crown Royal* rye whiskey from under the counter, handed it to him, and said, "Is this better? Merry Christmas." From that day forward all the windows and doors, bundles of lumber and shingles, and stacks of drywall had IRISH scribbled across them. Sub-trades commented how there never was much scrap on a Kiely site. My Father was a sought-after general contractor now, his days were long, and he said him and his crew were making money hand over fist.

I had some resentment towards my Dad for the move to the ten-acre lot on Highway 48 with the mailing address of R. R. #1 Cedar Valley that should have been Nowhere Land. While framing, I was holding two by fours for him, and I would write notes on them. I'd ask him questions, like "How much would you sell this house for?"

And he said, "One hundred and fifty thousand."

So I'd write, 'Sold! For one hundred and fifty thousand dollars' on my planks, and other stuff like 'My parents were mean for moving me to 'B.F.I - bum fuck Idaho'. Our only neighbours were forest, the highway, and the head of twenty-five to thirty cattle that kept the grass on the steep hills nipped down tight to the north of us. The cows had flies all over their faces and they would swish their short tails, grazing at steep seventy-five degree angles during the summer. They all grew fat and were long gone to market when the winter wind would create big drifts of snow. The wind was fierce at the top of the hill and could sometimes knock you off your feet. I must say, that after a good dump of fresh powder, with the exception of the odd rock or cow-patty, this place did have stellar tobogganing hills.

Once Dave Spang attempted to down-hill-ski in the cow field. It was his virgin flight. He had new gear and went straight down the hill a lot faster than he expected. He managed to remain standing until he stopped dead at the bottom of the big hill, snapping the ends off his skis. Uncle Dave picked himself and his broken gear up, and told everyone laughing to "Go fuck yourselves!" before he walked in those clunky boots all the way back to the house.

Even with all my chores I was dying of boredom at that charming age when 'you can do this, but you can't do that'. When you ask why, the answer is, "That's why."

In Grade Eight everyone was chewing packages of "Ton O' Gum" which was basically a giant slab of bubble gum that if mistakenly swallowed could prove life threatening. We could blow bubbles the size of our heads, and when it popped you did your best to keep it out of your hair. Really, this stuff should have come with warnings on the label: Chewers may choke, suffocate, or pull fillings during use.

Colleen had gotten an Easy Bake Oven for Christmas, and she was always baking these little cakes with a light bulb, for her, Sean, and Pixie. My sister just hated hot dogs, but one day for mischief I chopped up a piece of one really fine and put it into her cake batter when she wasn't looking. When Colleen bit into her cake, she spit it out crying, "Somebody put wieners in my cake!" My Mother immediately smacked my ass hard, and that pissed me off. Who said it was me? How did she know I put the wieners in the cake?

Mom said, "Come on, Pauline, I didn't do it. Your Dad isn't here. Sean says he didn't, and Jim couldn't have. I know I didn't. In a process of elimination that leaves you."

"I don't care. Maybe I didn't do it." I argued for argument's sake.

Over the next few weeks my Mother tried everything to bait me to confess to the crime of the wieners in the cake. Dad just kept insisting that at some point my tongue would turn black from the lie. About three weeks into the stand-off, Mom, Colleen, Sean, Jim, and I were at a variety store where our Mother said we could pick a treat, anything you want. So I reached for the Ton O' Gum.

My Mom said, "You really want that gum, don't you?"

"Yes." I said.

"Then admit it. Just admit you put the wieners in Colleen's cake."

"OK, OK," I said, "I put the freakin' wieners in the cake!"

Mom said, "You can have that gum, but you're grounded for two weeks."

What the hell else was new? It seemed I was always grounded for something. And we lived in the 'middle of nowhere anyway'.

My teacher's name was Miss Capaski. She had been educated in a Montreal convent, and rumour was she had at one time been a nun. Occasionally Miss Capaski would throw a piece of chalk my way, or slam her yard stick on my desk because I was that disruptive, impossible kid in the class. We had gotten brand new desks, but before the morning bell even rang, Annette and I had had a war and scribbled all over the tops of ours.

For Grades Seven and Eight I attended that little country five-room school called Our Lady of Good Counsel in the village of Sharon. Miss Capaski was likely the best teacher I ever had. She called me "Trouble". I caused her so much stress that she questioned, "Miss Kiely, would it be your mission in life to drive me insane?"

Miss Capaski was maybe thirty. She had a natural dirty blond Afro, and she wore bell bottoms with paisley prints and colourful scarves. Our little school didn't have a gym, but Miss Capaski put hours into coaching the Grade Eight girls' basketball team. We didn't figure we stood a chance, but she made practice fun. Annette, Liz, and I were the tall ones. Annette played forward, and Liz and me defence, but we didn't do it on our own because the rest of the girls in the class gave it everything too. We won the York Region Separate School Elementary Girls Basketball Championship in 1974.

At recess and lunch the Grade Eight girls would congregate behind the only tree, a crab apple tree, at the back of the school yard. We'd talk about the boys we had crushes on, and the changes happening to our bodies.

One spring Monday as we routinely went out to stand behind this tree we noticed plastic baggies with twist ties hanging in our tree. Once one was spotted there were more, maybe five, six, or even seven little bags tied to our tree. On closer inspection there was urine in these bags. When someone spotted the bag with some crap in it, we ran to tell the principal and Miss Capaski. We only had six boys in our class that year and out of the six, two were shy, two were cute, and two were disgusting.

On the home front Jim was still a little guy, and very entertaining. After dinner my Father would say, "Come over here, Jim, and I'll rascal you," and that meant he'd give him a tickle and a cuddle. Sometimes Jim would have to remind his Daddy, "You forgot to rascal me today."

One Saturday morning little Jim woke up, and I had an idea. I said, "Jim, you are still dreaming . . . you're not awake yet," and I was moving my arms to imitate floating. Colleen and Sean joined in and they agreed, "Jim, this is a dream. You're not awake. You can even go downstairs and tell Dad to truck off."

So this sweet little four-year-old in his little slippers and pj's goes downstairs and shouts at his Father what sounds like, "Hey, Dad, Fruck off." and gets a spank on the bum and sent back to bed. Stomping his way up the stairs, he shouts at us, "I hate you guys! This is not a dream!" And we are in hysterics.

Poor Jim, we would blindfold him and do taste testing. I told him when he could tell what he was eating without seeing it, he was a big boy. We fed him nice things like ice cream, honey, and peanut butter, but then it was hot mustard or Tabasco sauce. I was fourteen but we were buddies. He used to jump into my arms from the countertop in our kitchen.

Our new house was almost exactly the same layout as the old house in Ballantrae, except it was much larger. I believe twenty-five hundred square feet with an attached garage and full finished basement. In the basement we had a make-do kitchen while Dad made the fashionable knotty pine cupboards. This house was high on a hill, and was struck by lightning at the front left corner during framing. This time we didn't move into two by fours. We had the luxury of drywall, and doors with nails for knobs. Before long we had barn beams in our kitchen ceiling, and a cathedral cedar ceiling in the living room. The focal point, pretty much dead center in this house, was the floor-to-ceiling field stone fireplace, with an elevated giant hearth, and barn beam mantle. The neighbours in Markham had given my parents the gift of a bronzed crest, the Kiely's Crest, and this was proudly hung above the mantle.

While helping my Dad chisel stones for the fireplace in Ballantrae, Jerry Clancy had a rock nick his wrist. The blood spurted. They tied it off and went to Scarborough Hospital for stitches. I remember watching them - sometimes there would be sparks when the hammer hit the chisel and the chisel hit the rock. Blood just spurted straight up like the water fountain at school. A few drops of Jeremiah's blood would likely be on that fireplace forever. Doesn't this exact same thing happen to my Father while chiselling stones with him again on a Friday night, but this time they knew how to handle it. Apply pressure, and hold it; then clean it and bandage it! Although the performance was great, nine times out of ten the nick was so small it didn't require a stitch.

November of 1975 was a sad time for us indeed. My Aunt Kate, Uncle Dave, Tina, and Greg returned to Ireland to live. They had been staying at our house the last two weeks, and we got sort of used to them helping to fill up the big place. Last summer, while she balanced the books for Betz Pools, I had babysat Tina and Greg and become quite fond of them.

Greg was a fashionable little man sporting a little blonde surf cut. He and Jim would be playing on their *Big Wheels* in the driveway and Greg, who was fascinated by Batman, would sing;

Batman! Swings on a rubber band,
falls in a frying pan,

chases off the boogy man,
and puts him in a tin can,
Batman! Dan a na na na na na na na na Na! Batman!

Tina was younger than Sean but older than Jim, and liked to do her own thing. I would tease Jim, saying "Smile, bigger, bigger. Come on, you can do bigger than that." He was still a pre-schooler with dark curly hair, a freckle-spattered face, and sparky blue eyes. Colleen and Sean entertained themselves. They would bury treasures and make maps. Sean was a big 'Star Trek' fan. I never tired of 'The Flintstones'. My Father enjoyed Archie Bunker in 'All in the Family'. My Mother's favourite was 'Leave it to Beaver'. Colleen liked 'Gilligan's Island' and Jim hardly missed Ernie and Burt on 'Sesame Street'. We had an antenna, a rotor, and were doing well if we got reception on channels 3, 5, 7, 9, and 11 on the same day.

When Pixie was in Jimmy's old high chair Colleen said, "He's in Spy School" because she was Madame X, and Sean was Joe, and they were spies. She'd be wearing a black and white striped plastic rain coat and hat from one of Aunt Agnes's rummage sales. Her teeth were growing in and Sean's had been knocked out in a collision his face had had with a lamp pole in the driveway. Sean had a BB gun, and one day when Dad was walking around the pool he noticed BB marks on his windows. He shouted, "Sean, you little bugger, have you been shooting at my windows!"

And Sean said, "No, Dad, it was the bullet that ricocheted.

Another time Dad yelled, "Sean, you little bugger, have you been whacking the drywall with your hammer?"

My Mother said she was afraid to answer the phone because it was usually the school, and not with good news. I was in puberty and had gained weight again. I'd become a bit of a bully, and did nasty things like placing thumb tacks on people's chairs.

After a Knights of Columbus fundraising dance where Miss Capaski met my Father with a glow on, she said, "I have a much better understanding of where you're coming from now."

When Denis was seventeen, he came to live with us one summer to work as a labourer for my Father. My girlfriends were all goofy over my cute cousin in his faded tight jeans and platform shoes, but I certainly never saw him that way. Denis was like my brother. He still had energy when he came home from work and he'd blast his Led Zeppelin or Deep Purple Machine Head albums in his room. I'd go to my room and be blasting Elton John's Yellow Brick Road, or my Kiss Destroyer record. We played these albums over and over, day after day, until the day that my Dad said, "I just can't take it anymore." He knocked on my door, opened it, removed the record from the player and snapped it in half. Then he said, "The same shit droning again and again; it's like Chinese torture." Mom said Dad had a lot on his mind in those days: six big houses on the go in one summer. I knew he had water on the knee. He had a big crew working for him, and had to line up all the sub-trades like plumbers and electricians. He told me he lay awake all night when the concrete foundations were poured.

Chapter Nine

Go Big or Go Home

During adolescence when we lived at the ten-acre property near the village of Mount Albert I felt isolated. Our
new house was amazing, and only about five miles up
Highway 48 from Ballantrae. It was set on the south side on
high ground. Rolling green hills set the stage for stupendous
sunsets. The place was regularly lit with visitors on weekends,
but during the week there was no one to knock around with after
my one friend moved. For Grades Ten, Eleven, and Twelve, I
might as well have been living in the Sahara desert. I was ado-
lescent. It wouldn't really have mattered where I lived because I
was awkward, irritable, and discontent.

Annette Straver, my "Dutchie" best friend, was born on
November 11th, 1961, in Newmarket Hospital. Her family consisted of her father Leo, mother Cory, brothers Ken and Larry,
and her baby sister, Bernita. They lived one concession road over
on what was known as Centre Road which led directly into the
village of Mount Albert - Mount Albert being a TD Bank, grocery
store, drug store, doctor's office, dentist, convenience store-gas
station, laundry mat, car wash, and the Towne Restaurant. I got
to know Annette on our school bus to Our Lady of Good Counsel

School in Grades Seven and Eight; but alas, my best friend moved to Newmarket for Grade Nine and had a new best friend. The worst part was that when I slept over at her new house, I liked Dawn too. She was hilarious, and the three of us giggled all night. Annette was always sincere, honest, individual, and strong.

The Straver's swapped their Center Road farm for a house in Newmarket so their children could do sports, and join clubs after school. We'd miss their farm with its in-ground swimming pool that we used extensively in the summer. Mr. Straver had built it, and he did things right. He put sheets of Styrofoam on the ground under the liner, and kept the water crystal clean. Ken and his friends Steve Tolle and Kevin Brocolli (whose last name wasn't really Brocolli but that's what we called him), would be in the pool. Poor Brocolli had a crush on Annette. His acne freaked her out.

Annette and I would meet in the Tolle's cornfield until the corn got neck high; then we'd have to go around the road way. The 'Dutchie' lived on a farm that had a long driveway. Their barn was in front of their house so it was a very private setting. The Straver's had a spiral staircase. They also had this loony curly-haired black Bouvier dog on a chain. The way the dog's bangs covered his eyes, I don't think he could see. He just went around in circles barking his fool head off. The dopey dog weighed over a hundred pounds, so we made sure not to get in his way.

Mrs. Straver had a strong Dutch accent, and would call me Pauleenstia. She seemed to sing everyone's name. She made us melted Gouda on toast. Mr. Straver was an engineer. His tight curls were white. Annette had long thick straight gold hair, Ken was a stamp of his father, and Larry looked more like Annette. Little Bernita was a chatty brunette. She was in Sean's class, but Sean sat with Larry on the bus.

Around eight a.m. Colleen, Sean, and I faced all weather waiting at the end of our paved driveway that was lined with lights, shrubs and trees. We'd see it chugging up the road, that seventy-two seater, big yellow magic bus, with Annette, Larry, and Bernita the only passengers aboard. Ken went to Newmarket High on another bus, and we went to the little Catholic School in Sharon. The school bus was hollow, tinny, and cold. Our driver was a Scotsman about forty-five who didn't say much and rarely smiled. We'd catch Scotty checking on us with the eyes in the back of his head, the mirror, as the bus filled up.

Scotty was on a mission. Even when it had been raining or snowing, that dude just put the pedal to the metal. We'd be lifted off our seats going over bumps and railway tracks. It was always muddy on the back roads, and one morning I took the liberty of writing WASH ME in the dirt on the back window. Our driver had spotted me and appeared at the back of the bus, and the man lost it. He was shouting something, but his accent was so thick that I really couldn't make out what he was saying. I kept saying, "Pardon? Pardon? I don't understand you." Scotty's face got redder and madder until he got back in the bus and drove away. The Principal said I had to apologize, and promise not to write on the bus again. So I did, and I didn't.

Annette and I had gotten really close and I missed her very much. She got a real kick out of our family and the whole French and Irish thing. She said her family was 'a bit more normal'.

The funny story about Annette is that when she was born her family lived on Aurora Side Road in Ballantrae. Her birthday is two days before my friend Ruth Stickwood's birthday who still lived on Aurora Side Road. Turns out the two had been switched at birth for a whole day in the hospital, and it was Mrs. Straver and Mrs. Stickwood who finally said, "This isn't my baby" to the nurses. And then Annette was my friend, and Ruth was my friend, and they were introduced to each other at my house where they put the pieces together.

Our house was a sprawling ranch brick bungalow with blonde brick and a black roof and shutters. It had a full walkout basement, and was outfitted with an intercom system. My Mother's voice over the intercom was our alarm clock. One morning when I was in Grade Eleven, she said, "Good morning, Pauline, time to get up. Have you ever smoked paraquat pot?" I jumped up and answered, "No, why? Do you have some?" Mom wasn't amused because there were warnings on the radio about the tainted weed, and apparently this shit could kill you. The intercom system piped music through our house, and we could press a button and talk to one another, or answer the door if the doorbell rang. There was a game room for the ping-pong table, and an elaborate wet bar. My Father had built all this. It was his vision and ambition; and my Mother would say, "I just hang on to his coat tails." He would say, "Brute force and perseverance, Woman. We're a team of fine horses that pull together. When one grows tired, the other digs in."

Jim, John, and Yolande Kiely - 1973

Dad converted the laundry room into his dark room to develop his photos. He was taking a class, and we were all welcome to observe and take part. My Mother gave him an envelope of old negatives she had; so the pictures were sometimes a surprise. He developed a beauty of Mom's grandparents, and gave all her brothers and sisters a copy. Dad was ever so proud of the black-and-white he took of Jim in an archway when his teacher raved over it.

Jim Kiely - 1974

On Sunday nights our family sat around the kitchen table where our Father's teaspoon went ting, ting, tang, as it swirled and blended the milk and sugar in his strong tea. "Do you lot know the story of Finn McCool? He was said to be the bravest warrior in old Ireland. As a boy Finn was sent to study and serve an old wise man, a holy man. The pair of them were fishing off the shore of the river Shannon for the salmon of knowledge. The legend was that the one to eat this salmon would gain all the wisdom in the world. Well, doesn't the wise man catch the fish, and he asked Finn to clean it and cook it for him. So young Finn guts the fish, starts a fire, and places the salmon in the pan to cook. When he was flipping the fish, doesn't he burn his thumb; and when he stuck it in his mouth, sure enough, wasn't it young Finn who was the first to taste the salmon of knowledge, and wasn't it he who was destined to gain all the wisdom in the world. You do know what the moral of the story is? If you do the job, you gain the knowledge.

I fancied myself a bit like young Finn McCool. I had all the answers, and if there were waters to be tested I was the first one with my toe in. After tea we faithfully hit the couch to catch *Disney*. That would be followed by *The Irish Rovers*. We didn't have any neighbours, and my friends were long distance by phone and five miles south. It was a big break when I was transferred from the high school in Newmarket to Stouffville because that's where my buddies from Ballantrae were.

Towards the end of our horsing around, Laurie Wood was riding Anne Marie's horse Rusty. Ruthie grew out of her Shetland pony named Peanuts. For me, it was too late. As hard as my Father had tried, I'd noticed boys. My horse was lonely, and she started getting loose to visit a lone Paint-horse down the highway. I explained to Jet that I loved her very much, and thanked her for the friendship and the adventures over the years. I needed a life and new transportation so we sold her, and used the money to buy a ten speed bicycle. My Father shed tears.

My career as a kid was coming to an end. During summer holidays, after chores, I'd ride my bike down to Ballantrae. Other days my Mom took pity on me and would drive me down to Cauldin's on Lake Road. She'd have a mug of java and a chinwag with Mrs. C. This would be our drop-off and meeting place. I was let loose on the world until eleven p.m. sharp once or twice during the week. I hung out with Bryan and Amy. Once in a while I'd bring my friend Janet from Bogart town, and we'd walk around Musselman's Lake. It's not a big lake, more of a glorified pond; so the walk wasn't a big deal. Janet and I could last all day on an ice-cream sandwich.

Carousel Variety was the first stop, but if nobody was around we just carried on down to Glendale Beach cause that's where everybody hung out. There was a foosball table, pinball machines, and the juke box. We were all big Bob Seger and Rolling Stones fans; but disco was in and whenever K.C. and the Sunshine Band sang, "Do a little dance, make a little love, get down to-night!", we all shouted, "Get down the Ninth!" because The Lake road connected with the Ninth Line at the top of the hill. Brucie Bingham would get up and do *the robot*.

This was the center of the universe! I thought I had a crush on Brucie's brother, Frankie, because he was taller and the seventh son. My Mother kept insisting that there was an old wives' tale about the seventh son being lucky, but Frankie was cranky, so I stuck with Bruce who was gangly, freckly, with blue eyes and a dark brown feathered haircut. His father Hughie hid from his wife, 'Wee Jean', in their garage sipping beers.

Mr. Bingham said, "Blackie, you've got a buxom beauty there." But I wasn't sure this was a compliment. I probably had twenty pounds on his lad, 'Brucie Bing-Ham without the cheese'. Bruce was the sixth of seven boys and one girl. His buddy Robbie was one of a litter of thirteen. Apparently Robbie's father had installed a chain and pad-lock around their fridge, and he said his phone number was 000-0000 because he didn't have a phone.

Brucie would talk to anyone. He would tell older women he was a Boy Scout, and offer them his arm to cross the street. All the while Mister Personality would be complimenting them about their scarf, brooch, or hair-do. He'd hold the door for people and say, "Welcome to the Glendale Beach Pavilion," as if it were his place and he was the ambassador. The old dance hall had seen better days. It sure could have done with a lick of paint, but the pop and chips were cheap and the memories priceless.

I remember one Saturday night there was a dance band in the house. You had to be eighteen to get in. The real owners, the Edwards, knew none of us were eighteen; so there was no point in even trying to fake it. We were just hanging around the concrete fountain near the parking lot when a member of the band came outside with a bucket. He dumped this lump of dry ice into the water of the fountain. The water began to smoke and smoulder. Robbie picked up the puck of ice, and he immediately tossed it in the air screaming, "This fucking ice burns!"

I played baseball and hung out with Ruth Stickwood, Laurie Wood, Laurie Lockhart, and Karen Milligan. All these girls lived in the sub-division except Ruthie who lived on a one-acre lot like us. Ruth's dad, Cecil, was a part-time auctioneer that worked full time on the roads. Her mother Margie sang in the choir and helped out at Churchill Church. Cec would let Ruth and Annemarie drive his truck on the back roads. He gave his 'little Ruthie' and 'princess Annemarie' everything he could. One Saturday Mr. Stickwood gave 'his little girls' this old Ponti-ac that they drove around their back pasture in circles. When the car died it remained parked near the garage, and it became our club house. We sat in it and talked, and smoked a joint if we scored. We knew we were *cool.* Some of the guys said they were biker wanna-be's. We learned to be careful what you wish for be-cause real bikers moved into the area; and in a couple of years what was for fun was now for real.

Ruth's older sister, Annemarie, was beautiful. She had waist-long, sable brown, wavy hair and indigo eyes. Ruth was petite and just as pretty only without the hair. Ruthie, Laurie, and Karen were all about the same size, small. Laurie Lockhart was taller and more round, and I was a husky five nine.

My Uncle Dan was our baseball coach one season. He drove an orange Roadrunner muscle car that had *The Beach Boys* singing on an 8-track tape. His car smelled like Bruté co-logne. Dan looked a lot like *Guess Who* singer, Burton Cum-mings. I had no idea that a couple of the girls had a bit of a crush on him until I picked up on Paula Henshaw at a game.

"Dan is such a sweet guy; he even married that woman with the speech impediment." Sometimes Brenna came out to the games with their little lad, Jacob, who would push his plastic lawnmower behind the stands. I said, "Speech impediment. His wife doesn't have a speech impediment. That's an Irish accent."

I was up to bat at a game in Goodwood, and this yap on the other team kept saying, "No batter, no batter, no batter."

I shouted, "Hey, are you blind? I'm a batter here, and you can pucker up, sweetheart, and kiss my Royal Canadian!" and then I slapped my own ass. She shut her gob, but as only fate would have it, on that Goodwood team was Paula Perry, the daughter of Mr. Jerry Perry, owner of Rainey Transport, for whom my Father had built three homes in Bristol Ponds. Dad came home from work a few days later and said, "I heard all about your Royal Canadian today."

Ruthie was in my class. Princess Annemarie was seventeen when she got married to Mark because they were pregnant. I admired her courage. Things went sour fast with Mark because he went to jail. They split up, and she had this little fella that we all fussed over. Soon after, Annemarie had a new boyfriend, a big German whose chin stuck out when he spoke with authority, and she was safe from Mark. This new couple were so cute together; he had to pick her up to kiss her because Annemarie is five-one, and Ferdinand is six-three.

One night we were buzzed out on home-grown, and Laurie Lockhart had us on the edge of our seats with one of her gory, gripping stories when Ruthie's calico cat, Mini-Tink, came up through a hole in the floor of the Pontiac and jumped onto Karen's lap. We screamed and laughed so loud that house lights flicked on all over the place.

My friends were always welcome at our house. When Laurie Lockhart was given the keys to her mint green Rambler, she could drive the girls up for a swim. Once some of the guys overheard us talking, and asked if they could come swimming. I said, "Sure," never taking them seriously or expecting they'd really drive all the way out to my house.

We were all in the pool horsing around, and I heard the intercom door bell bing-bong but paid no attention. The next day at school Frank, Barry, and Doug cornered me, and Jay Thomas says, "So we met your Father last night! Hell of a nice guy."

I was surprised, "You came to my house?"

"Oh ya," Jay said, "Frank borrowed his mother's car, and we pooled our money for gas and drove up to your house. We rang the bell, and when your Father answered the door, he said, 'Can I help you?' And I explained, "I am Jay, this is Barry, Frank, and Doug. We are friends of Pauline's. Is she home?"

Your Dad said, "You boys appear to be lost. Have you been drinking? I don't know any Pauline. She doesn't live here." and he slammed the door.

"Oh, my God, guys, I'm so sorry. I'll have to have a chat with my Dad."

That evening during dinner I asked, "Did anyone come to the door last night?"

"As a matter of fact, a motley crew of drunkards with towels under their arms came to the door, but I thought they were lost." he said.

"Dad, those are my friends. Why would you do that?"

"The girls are welcome for a swim anytime. Why do you have to ruin everything with the boys? Jesus, Pauline, how can I fecking relax in my own house with a horny bunch of bowsies in my pool?"

He went to the sales barn and now we had a hobby farm, and the animals were grazing out of their pasture space. When my Father needed some fence posts dug, he put the job out for tender to those boys who came to the house to go for a swim, because sometimes *those boys* drove me home on occasion. My Old Man said we had to move from Ballantrae because he had visions of me marrying a biker.

"Any of those bums looking for a job?" he asked.

Jay took on the challenge. It was honest work digging post holes by hand in the heat while being eaten alive by bugs in the bush.

John Kiely fencing - 1975

My Mother made homemade wine, so we had a stocked wine cellar. One Friday night I helped myself to a bottle. I put it in a bag, and then into my big purse. I had my purse over my arm when I opened Laurie Woods' screen door. It swung, hit the glass, and shattered it.

Mrs. Wood was shocked and asked, "Pauline, what do you have in that purse? A brick!"

I said, "No, just some junk. Honestly, I'm so sorry."

Then we left and went to Karen's to drink the vino.

Mr. and Mrs. Wood appeared to have a perfect family. Mrs. Wood was curvy, and she had a gentle voice and warm eyes. They'd had five children over a span of twenty years. Her husband called her Lorna, and she always was nicely dressed.

Tom Wood was tall and slim and generally wore a dress or golf shirt. He was a vibrant upstanding member of the community who enjoyed reading one thing after another, sitting cross-legged under a lamp.

One day Laurie and I were washing their car. An elderly neighbour couple with their terrier dog asked her to hold onto Surf while they passed. Surf was a big white Shepherd. Laurie's voice was all sugar and spice, "Sure, Mr. and Mrs. Calvert, no problem. It sure is a beautiful day." Once they passed, she let go of Surf and said, "What I wanna say is, "No, you old bag; and Surf, eat that rat." and we laughed.

The next time my parents went on about the lovely Laurie Wood, I told this story. From that day forward Laurie Wood was lovingly referred to as Eddie Haskell by Mr. Kiely - Eddie Haskell being the lad on *Leave It to Beaver* who was always sweet in front of June and Ward Cleaver, but pulling some sort of prank or causing trouble when they weren't looking.

Laurie Lockhart and I met in a biology class in Grade Ten. Her parents, Howie and Marg, were older but *so cool.* They'd had their daughter late in life and were very soft on her, and patient with us. Laurie, Karen, Ruth, and I would be at Lockhart's playing euchre when her folks were and weren't home. They often spent weekends at the cottage. We had parties when we promised we wouldn't have parties. Sometimes things got a bit out of control because I got on the phone and invited some of "The Lake" boys over.

We met Steve Milmine through Laurie Lockhart. Steve had frizzy hair, and tons of patience. He took on the role of our chauffeur and never appeared bothered by our high-pitched voices when he squealed the tires of his red Malibu. We never wore seatbelts, and he regularly pushed that car past a hundred miles an hour to clean out the exhaust.

Laurie Lockhart had dreams and ambitions. She was taking biology because she wanted to be a nurse. I took biology because I was impressed by X and Y chromosomes. When it came to dissecting baby pigs, worms, or rabbits, I couldn't do it. It turned my stomach. As much as Lockhart tried to cover for me, I failed that class.

I had no idea what I wanted to be but completely identified with the character Mary Clancy that Hailey Mills portrayed in the 1966 classic film, 'The Trouble with Angels'. Even though Mary had the best of intentions, she and her sidekick Rachel, always managed to get into some sort of lobster pot at The St. Francis Academy School for Girls. They get caught smoking in the washroom, and on a road trip Rachel falls in love with a cowboy. In the end, the wild Hailey appears to be tamed and decides to dedicate her life to God and prayer and become a nun.

I thought for a while about what it would be like to be a nun, a servant of God, and I had visions of abstinence and solitude, the only sounds being murmured prayers and hymns. The scent of incense and candles and big cathedrals came to mind when I thought about this vocation. Then I thought again, and figured I'd already blown the interview as I'd broken a few Commandments. It was just a flash idea really, after my heart being touched by the film, like the flash I had about being shy. I'd tried that once too, and realized it takes a heap of patience to be shy, patience I didn't appear to have.

I remember being very obvious when I liked a boy in school. I wasn't a stalker or anything, but I'd gush if he looked my way or talked to me. My Mother says I wear my heart on my sleeve. I'm an open book. That's why they always knew when I was up to something. I should have told her I wanted to become a nun for April Fool's Day. She'd have come back with something like, "Perfect, then you'd be a Holy, Holy Terror."

Somebody was watching out for me though because one Saturday night I lied to my parents and told them I was staying at Laurie Lockhart's. Really I had plans to go to a big biker party at Wagon Wheel Ranch. The girls in the subdivision were not so daring, but I was perilous.

The main party was in a hall built under a new storage barn. Anne and Ferdi were there, Brucie and Robby, Delsey, Joey, Amy, and Mike. So I knew some faces. I'd had a few drinks and a couple of tokes but was still a virgin, all show, no go. I was wobbly so I went outside for some fresh air. There were a lot of people there, a lot of bike clubs - Hell's Angels, Paradise Riders, Black Diamond riders. It was a heavy-duty crowd. One bearded beast grabbed my arm and said, "Sweetheart, have you ever seen a pink bunny?"

I shook my head no, and he put his arm around my back and was guiding me towards the barn saying, "Just wait until you see the pink bunny, honey." When we got to the barn doorway, Brucie Bingham was there. He says to this guy, "Where do you think you're going? This one's with me." He grabbed my arm, spun me around, and said, "Walk fast."

So I did and we went back inside and sat next to Brucie's brothers, Horn, Jack, and Pad. They were sitting with Ferdi, and the big guy we called 'Puff'. Then Bruce said, "I might have just saved your life. There are no pink bunnies, you dummy. That's what they tell you before they rape you." Bruce saved me, and I remembered the story of the girl who went to the dance.

Life is an incredible journey, and it takes all kinds of flowers to make a beautiful garden. When the time comes for me to meet my Maker, I hope that He and I can sit in a peaceful place, and He can show me what I did right and where I went wrong. From my heart will beam thanks, thanks for my guardian angel. Thanks for all of it.

Chapter Ten

Sharp as a Tack

I had viewed a film about elderly people living on the streets, and the lonely old folks in nursing homes. It was so sad. It ate at me for days, but I didn't really know any old people. Sure I was surrounded by a great big family, but nobody was old. The only old person I could think of was my Granny in Ireland, the one I had peed on when I was seven. So I found her address in Mother's black book; Mrs. Elizabeth Kiely, 3 St. Patrick's Road, Dalkey, County Dublin, Ireland, and I began writing her letters.

Our house was active enough so I dropped an envelope in the mail once a week, or at the very least, three times a month. Once I enclosed an herbal tea bag which apparently didn't go over very well. Aunt Kate wrote me back to say that it was very nice of me to write Granny, and that she did enjoy the letters, but I should know that her mother said she wouldn't be caught dead drinking feckin' fruity foreign tea.

The letters became known as *The Perils of Pauline*. My Granny read my words to the cousins, Uncle Pat, Aunt Kate, and Maggie. Maggie is only eight years older than me so I've never come around to calling herself "Auntie". Granny told Dad that the girls in the Post Office made a fuss when her Canadian Air-mail arrived. She had to go around and collect her mail as it wasn't delivered to a tin box at the end of the driveway like ours.

Dad had gone back to the *Old Sod* pretty much every year for a three week visit generally in September, the eighth being his mother's birthday, and the twelfth his own. He'd return to us fattened up by soda bread, blood pudding, and gallons of Guinness. He'd be topped up with new stories for teatime.

So I felt like I sort of knew herself and my cousins: Kerry, and his brother Michael the Archangel, with their blister sister Tess who at times tortured the youngest, little Orla. Tess was a big Elvis fan; and after touring Graceland in Memphis, Tennessee, my Father posted her a card and signed it Lisa Marie. There was no problem in my telling it like it was.

> *Dear Granny,*
>
> *I was at the table the other day when your son came in and said, "I'm so hungry I could eat a boiled child's arse through a cane back chair." It was already dark outside because it's winter here.*
>
> *His face was all red and his glasses steamed up when he came into the kitchen, and he said "It's so cold out there I had to kick the ice out from under the dog."*
>
> *My mother was cooking. She had asked us what we wanted for dinner, and Sean and I both said, "Spaghetti!" cause we love the stuff.*
>
> *Dad asked, "What's for dinner?"*
>
> *Mom answered, "Spaghetti."*
>
> *And he said, "Yolande, does my face look feckin' Italian to you? I'm Irish, woman. For Christ's sake, cook me some cabbage and potatoes."*
>
> *Once he ate something he was in better form. The following day my Mother cooked him a pile of cabbage and potatoes, and he asks, "Where's the meat? The joint of ham or corned beef?"*

She said, "You didn't say anything about meat!" We were eating our pizza. So he ate his cabbage and potatoes, and had some of our pizza too.

> *Hope this finds you well.*
> *Love and best wishes,*
> *Pauline*

I had the time to write to Granny, and I wrote whatever tickled my fancy on her son's letterhead. I was confident in doing so because of the stories my Father had told me about his mother when those two heaping spoons of sugar went *plip plop*, and his spoon chimed as it bounced off the inside edges of his steaming china cup. My Father insisted, "Red Rose tea is the best."

He said, "There are no flies on my Mother. One evening she and I were on our way home after being at a local. Yer man, Joe Murphy, was out sweeping his walk. In passing he says, 'Evenin', Mrs. Kiely. Sure hasn't it turned very cold?'

"And says she to him, 'Joe Murphy, you've a fine fat wife in there to keep you warm. I shouldn't t'ink you'll be mindin' the cold.'

"Kate told me, 'Maggie's husband, Charlie, gave Mammy this lovely collie dog named Dusty. The only trouble was Dusty chases motorbikes. This young lad goes by on his rat-ta-tat Suzuki motor-bike, and doesn't Dusty go mad after him. So the young lad comes back with a stick with a nail in it, and he's going to hit Dusty. My Mother gives the young lad a smack in the gob and tells him, 'Feck off with yourself! Who the hell do you t'ink you are, beatin' other people's dogs?'

"Doesn't the young lad complain to the Guarda; and, Jesus, wasn't poor Mammy devastated when the Police came and took her Dusty away."

Dad went on, "You remember how in Ireland they have that gas meter in the kitchen and they put the money in as they go when they use it?" I nod yes.

"Well, your Granny figured out that it runs on holy medals; so if she hasn't any shillings she uses the holy medals.

"Apparently one day yer man from the gas knocks on her door, and yer man asked her, 'Is the man of the house at home today, Mrs.?'

"And she answered, 'No.'

"Yer man inquired, 'When might you be expecting him then?'

"And she said, 'I don't.'

"So yer man asks, 'Where is he then?'

"And says she, 'I believe he's taken a job in hell shovelling coal!' and shuts the door."

Elizabeth Kiely - 1978

It was June in '78 when Brenna was going back to Ireland to show her babies Jacob and Alicia to her Mammy, and enjoy a cup-o-cha with her sisters.

The Spangs bought a house on Killiney Hill which was a stone's throw to Dalkey. Aunt Kate hadn't been impressed with winters in Canada. Even though she had the best of sheepskin coats and all the gear, she simply could not take those January and February sub-zero freezing temperatures. She had a bad case of cabin fever in the winter, and an almost allergic reaction to mosquito bites in the summer. It would appear this Irish Colleen came to Canada for a Canadian! She found one; had the perfect family, a girl and a boy, didn't care for the climate, so emigrated back.

The Gildeners had been at our place in Mount Albert when Brenna mentioned she was going to visit her mother, and my Father said without thinking, "Yolande, would you like to go to Ireland?"

And Mom was quick to reply, "I'd love to go to Ireland, John."

Barb and Len Cauldin were over. It was the usual Saturday night crowd. The Cauldin's had met Granny when she was over for Brenna and Dan's wedding. Mrs. Cauldin asked, "Can I go to Ireland?"

And my Father said, "Do you have a passport, Barbara Cauldinski? Buy your ticket. I don't see why not."

Ice tinkled in tumblers that clanked during toasts, "Cheers! Down the hatch", or "Here's to your health." Dad was wearing his hair longer, and he had some grey hairs now. He had sideburns, a mustache, and wore thick, tinted wire-frame glasses. On Saturday night he might wear his powder blue suit with a polyester shirt, or sometimes these nasty plaid pants. Mom wore a white jumpsuit with a zipper up the front and silver chain belt. She strapped her little feet into little silver shoes. Their gang would gather at our place. Whoever showed up would have a drink or two, and then they would car pool to a dance or up to a pub called *The Irish House* in Jackson's Point. *The Irish*

House was owned by a wee man from Belfast called Johnny Watson. He and Dad had an agreement that *the troubles* could stay across the pond. There would be live music in his establishment, and my folks and their friends were regulars.

I would go out on Friday nights, and be asked to babysit for them most Saturday nights. While they were out, I'd prepare a cheese and cracker tray or make a plate of sandwiches, and set up the coffee pot as everyone generally came in for a night cap. The men usually had a good glow on, with my Father being the loudest. I'd roll over at the sound of their voices and laughter, and I'd hear my old man singing;

> *"One has hair of silvery grey the other has hair of gold.*
> *One is young and beautiful, and the other is bent and old.*
> *These are the two that are dear to me,*
> > *from them I never will part.*
> *One is my mother, God bless her,*
> > *I love her . . . and the other is my sweetheart."*

So my Mother, Aunt Brenna with Jacob and baby Alicia, plus Barb Cauldin jetted off to Dublin. Apparently they had arrived just in time. Granny had a broken denture, and her wild hair was in need of a cut and colour.

She was delighted with the company and Mrs. Cauldin returned with this story:

"It was wonderful. I've never felt more at home. I enjoyed myself from the moment we landed. *Busy Lizzy* and I got along famously. We had a bit of skit going. She kept insisting she wanted to buy me a present for coming to see her. So for a joke nearer the end of the holiday I'd spotted this expensive watch in an antique shop window. I pointed it out to her and said, 'Well now, Lizzy, there it is. There's the present you can buy me.'

And so says she to me, 'I tell what I'll do. I'll sign me life insurance over to you; go in, ask the price, drop dead, and the watch is yours.'"

Barb Cauldin had been Barb Tully. Her mother was Irish, and Mrs. C laughed from the belly and dabbed at tears when she told her stories: stories about growing up as one of seven tough Tully's in Willowdale, stories about how she learned to paddle her own canoe, and how she'd give you a number nine right between the thighs, number nine being her shoe size.

Dad loved hearing his wife talk about her trip. He encouraged her to think for herself and have a sense of humour. "Chin up, look on the bright side" was his motto. Besides, what was there not to like about my Mother. She made the most of everything, everyday; and if we complained she'd say "It's better than a slap on the belly with a wet fish."

Every so often he'd remind us, "Did you wake up in a clean bed this morning, and find your clean knickers, socks, and clothes folded in your drawers? Are we not enjoying a bite to eat, thanks to yours truly? Except for the smokes, my wife's perfect."

Brenna was still a little weak from having her babies. She was glad for the extra hands.

I was needed at home to mind the house while our Mother was away. I even got to drive her snazzy Cougar LTD. It had three windows down each side, and was dark brown with a sort of gold hard top. A big car that my friends said was way too big for my Mother. Turns out it was too big for me too. I had Colleen, Sean, and Jim in this car when we were pulling up to the pumps for some fuel. Before we got our gas, our car sort of whammed into a cement pole that indicates you're too close to the pumps. This put a neat crease above the front wheel on Colleen's side, and she said, "Dad is going to kill you."

When we got home, where was he? Only down at the barn chopping heads off chickens! Of all the days! My Father was trying his hand at farming, and had raised fifty meat birds. I calmly walked up to him and waved to get his attention.

"I need to talk to you about something. Dad, remember that dent at the front that Mom put in the car backing out of the garage?"

He said, "Yes, why . . ."

I said, "How much did it cost to fix? I had a little accident when we were getting gas."

He turned and walked towards his car and I followed him, noticing the chicken blood on his big hands, and especially the right hand which still had the bloody hatchet in it. He walked up to the car and looked at the dent, and looked at me, and looked at the dent, and me, and shouted, "I am cursed. Fuckin' cursed I tell ya! What was it, only eight months ago I fixed the exact same dent? Seven hundred and fifty bucks, Pauline, that's how much this costs." Then he turned and almost ran back towards the barn, swinging the hatchet and cursing. I went inside to make lunch and to show Colleen that I was still alive. Later that day my Dad was having a few beers, and he asked me for a smoke. I felt sorry for him. It had been a long two weeks; so I pulled my DuMaurier ciggies from my sock, and we puffed away on the filthy things together.

He called himself a gentleman farmer. We had the chickens, a pair of ducks, Colleen's Appaloosa horse named Kella, and Kella's old friend, Buck, Jim's pony. My Father had his Angus cows, Gay-lass and Wee-lass, and a spotted cow called Funny Face, plus the grey one he named Rene Leveque because the grey reminded him of the smoke swirling and curling around Monsieur Leveque during televised debates.

There was lots of controversy on the news. A Quebec separatist group called the F.L.Q. was challenging our Premier, Pierre Elliot Trudeau. My Father said they were separate-tits! I had gone to the Science Center with my friend Janet when this happened. I arrived home that evening and there was about an inch of fresh wet snow. I could see my family's footprints from the car to the house. Mom said, "Your Father and Sean had an accident today. They were towing a log up the hill from the valley with the Dexter tractor for firewood. When they got to the bottom of the hill, your Dad says to Sean, 'You'd better jump down, Son. This looks a bit dangerous.' While Sean was walking up the hill he heard the tractor rev; so he turned around and he saw the log caught on a tree and the tractor flip over. He's only eight, but he knew enough to run down to the tractor and dig in the dirt to uncover his Dad's face so he could breath. He said he had to help him turn his head to the side. That's what saved him! It's a good thing our Sean is such a fast runner because he ran up to the house as fast as he could, and gasping, managed to tell me to call an ambulance. It was awful, the weight of the tractor on your Father. His face was purple and then he went grey. I thought for sure I was going to lose him and I thought, 'You bastard, don't you leave me a widow like my mother.'

Colleen went out on the highway to flag down some help. People stopped because she was crying. Some men came and tried using their car jacks to relieve some weight. Then a tow truck arrived, and then finally the ambulance. The tow truck pulled the tractor off him just as the paramedics ran down the hill. When your Dad cracked a smile, and said, "Sean, get a load of *Rampart* coming down the hill?" *Rampart* like on TV! I knew if he was cracking jokes, chances were he was going to be alright. After the paramedics checked his vitals, they laid a stretcher next to him, and your Father said, "I'm very heavy, boys. I'll walk up."

But the man in charge said, "I don't think so, Mr. Kiely," and they carried him up to the ambulance, and took him to Newmarket Hospital where they're going to keep him for a couple of days."

When we went to visit Dad the next day he was pale and visibly shaken. The Doctor said that he had squished a vertebra in his spine, squished his left thumb, and was a very lucky man to be alive, as not many would have survived an accident like that one. My Da says to the Doc, "That was a close call. I saw the angels comin', but asked God for another chance. I've got a young family."

Then Mom burst into tears and said, "I had a vision of myself a widow, and asked God for another chance too."

Chapter Eleven

Happy New Year

I only saw my Mother furious once. Somehow my Dad, being the life of the party, ended up naked in a swimming pool with someone else's wife. In his defence this 'tart' chose to strip and jump in after him. This 'tart' telephoned our house. Apparently she was proud of their performance, and when my Father hung up, he looked at my Mother and said, "What's the matter with you? You're up and down like a whore's drawers on payday." And she lost it.

"I am disgusted with you, John Kiely! I don't know what kind of marriage you have, but your wife certainly doesn't go swimming in the skin with someone else's husband. Come on, how would you like it? Put the shoe on the other foot."

"Lovey, I'm sorry. I was a drunken fool. You know I'd never cheat on you, for Christ's sake. Look what that did to my family." He said, "For the life of me I don't understand why a man cheats on his wife. He loses everything for a piece of ass, when on the hole it's all the same."

My Mother had stitched together a brown vest with matching culottes for me that Christmas before my first adult New Year's Party. I wore a plaid Levis brand shirt under this vest that matched this popular style of knee length slacks meant to be worn with boots. I could wear make-up now, and puff on cigarettes in public. I was asked to go to the adult New Year's Party at Uncle Gill's in 1976, and felt good in my stylish outfit. Jeannette would be there, and it wasn't like I had other plans.

Uncle Ross said the economy was bust back in the 1940's. "People were walking away from their farms. Gill had a deal with the government that if he cleared and farmed fifteen acres of bush he'd get the deed to one hundred and sixty acres of land. He had to throw in some money, but it wouldn't have been much more than a couple of hundred bucks. To his credit, Gill met the criteria. It wasn't easy because back then five hundred bucks was a lot of money. Sometimes we'd all go up north, and give him a hand, but he pretty much did the bulk of work on his own. You've got to hand it to Gilbert. Where there's a will, there's a way."

Our family got what my Mother called 'the Newfie Christmas tree' from Uncle Gill's. It is very rough and rocky country there. He could maybe have a wild blueberry farm. His land is loaded with the fruit-bearing shrubs. You'd have to pack a pistol for snakes and vermin though. Also included on the deed and title are the rights to most of the west side of Lower Sturgeon Lake. This prime real estate is just north of their hometown where evergreens are tall, and Northern Pike and Walleye fishes are plenty in dark sapphire waters.

Uncle Gill had built a modest, cosy, two-storey house on his property. The house was grey roll brick and heated with wood. Fresh water was hand-pumped at the sink from the well. He had black and blue tin dishes. I was quite interested in how he survived here. He fed the fire and told me, "In the evenings I light propane lanterns, and I bake my own bread in this oven. The chemicals in the food these days. It is poison, this stuff. Me, I eat some things like in a restaurant dere, and I feel sick, me."

My Uncle Gill wasn't much bigger than my Mother. He was lean muscle. His coarse grey hair was buzzed short. He said, "I feel better these days, me, but I still wear this belt here, this, on my back when I work in the garden. My heels, they can still bodder me sometimes, even so many year after the accident, you know, that one where, me, I fall from the ladder."

Yolande Kiely and Gilbert Beaulieu - 1976

Out of bins of sawdust in his root cellar he pulled up turnips, potatoes, carrots, beets, and onions that he had grown in his garden that season. There also was what he called a cold cellar that housed jars of preserves, pickles, and canned things.

He said, "My Modder, she would make this dish at Christmas time. We call it 'Stew-poy,' Like Stew-pie for you English there. This pie it was maybe eight to ten inches tall, this pie. It was layers of like carrots, and then beaver, and then parsnips, and venison, and onions, and then partridge, and then potatoes, and then rabbit or pheasant, and turnips, then like the pie crust, you know, over the top of this and it was baked slow in the oven . . . and it was beautiful."

Uncle Gill had a few goats in the barn. He made soap, yogurt, and cheese from their milk. He carved leather for a hobby, and showed me some belts and purses he had in the works. He said he read a lot, and told me, "Last fall I have this big bull moose, he come down my driveway, and a few spring ago I see dese, a black bear with two cubs." My Mother's eldest brother had been kicked in the mouth by his father's horse when he was a young lad resulting in his bottom teeth being more prominent than his top teeth when he smiled. He wore black rimmed glasses, and always smiled. According to my Father, Uncle Gill was "one tough little Frenchman who should have been a bull fighter."

The dry cold fresh air up north tickled the end of my nose, sort of like how ginger ale bubbles do, and the heat of each breath was clearly visible before being consumed by the cold. Hard packed snow squeaked and crunched loudly underfoot. When I remained still, I was embraced by silence and beauty. A virgin white blanket rested over the wilderness where giant pines, cedar, and hemlock slept under the weight of the crystallized water. The warble of a chickadee broke the afternoon silence. The sky was true blue, and long icicles glistened as they dripped over the entrance of his home where smoke bellowed from a stove pipe.

After going around the room hugging and kissing my Aunts and Uncles, I was glad to take my place with my cousins Jeannette, Chris, Denis, and Reggie Dionne. When the French songs broke out, my Father said, "Your Mother's in her glory." and she was. Her cousin Ami came by for a visit. He was a burly bald man with big hands that copped a bit of a squeeze when he hugged hello. When I called him on it, he said he couldn't help himself because God made women so beautiful. My Mother said she was sorry she forgot to warn me about this cousin 'with the Roman hands and Russian fingers,' her mischievous cousin who she said looked the most like her father. Ami was famous for squeezing women, and also for the New Year's Eve he brought a deceased Uncle's corpse inside from the barn for a dance. That was when my Mother was a child. "In the winter when the ground was frozen they had to store a body somewhere until spring." Mom said, "Ami was a wild one that sometimes had too much moonshine."

Ami sat down next to me and said, "I hear you like the horses."

"I love them," I answered.

"You must get that from your grandfadder. He, him had the finest horse around. Your grandfadder, he have dis horse he name King. It was the strongest horse around, this King. People, dey come, dese people, for miles to breed to King cause he win all the competitions he goes in. Dis King is one of those Canadien's, dis horse. You hear of dese horses? Dis bishop, him, dis Bishop Louis from France, he, him, he give dese black horses special to the pioneers. Your Grandfadder, he have one of dese horses."

"One winter dis family with deir cutter, dey think dere, dat dey can take dis short cut across the river to get to Mass. But deir cutter it goes trew the ice, and dis family, dey are stranded out dere in the freezing water. I am just a kid, an altar-boy at dis time, me. People, dey are crying and thinking how to save dese people out dere. Dese women, dey are on their knees and praying, and some voice it is inside me, it says 'Ami . . . you must run and get Mon Unc Eugene, and his great horse King.' So I run as fast as I can to his farm, and I find him. He was milking a cow, so I says to him, 'Mon Unc, you must come quick', and I tell him about dese people, dere, so he comes to the river with me."

"When we got back dere is a big crowd, you know? Dey have trown dese people a rope, and dey have dis rope, it is tied to their cutter. Dese people on the shore, dey are pulling on dis rope, but it does nothing. The water was only maybe four to five feet deep, but dere were small children, and the current, she is fast. Your Grandfadder, he takes charge, and he says, "Untie dat rope!" And he pulled dis to himself, and he tie a few knots in dis rope, maybe two feet apart. Den he trow dis rope back to dat man, and he says to him and his wife, 'Hold on tight to da small ones, and all youse odder ones, you hold on very tight.'"

"Dis family, dey have maybe five or six kids. Dey are standing on the seats of deir cutter, and deir horse, it is moaning with pain before it go down. Then I hear Mon Unc Eugene, he count to tree and he tell King to, "Pull! Pull! Pull! and King, he Pull! Pull! Pull! and dis whole family dey come to the shore hanging on to dat rope dere. Dis man, he, him, he lost his horse and cutter, but dis man he remain forever grateful to your Grandfadder and his horse King." He took a deep breath, and his eyes leaked before cousin Ami finished his story.

Uncle George drank stubby bottles of Labatt's 50 warm. My Father enjoyed his Carlsberg cold, and Uncles Ross and Oscar got along. They'd agreed on Molson Golden from a fridge or cooler. My Father said Uncle George drank deer piss.

Agnes Tripp, Doloris Villeneuve, Yolande Kiely, Bette Dionne

Five, four, three, two, one . . . HAPPY NEW YEAR! And there was noise, hugs, well wishes, resolutions, and kisses. Jeannette and I made a pact that we would try and get together for a weekend once a month all year the whole New Year. We named the pact, 'The Trend.' We were tight. We had started smoking together when we were twelve and fourteen. For all I know there may still be a black package of Peter Jackson's buried on the north side of that big old maple tree in their back yard at 3 Byng Avenue.

Uncle Gill's neighbour Curtis showed up at our party late. He was three sheets to the wind, and he kept saying stuff to my cousin Reggie. He had his arm hanging around Reggie's neck and was saying something to him in French. My Mother made out what Curtis was slurring, and she said, 'Something about that Johnny Dionne being a fag because he has no body hair, and him, that Johnny Dionne, he is groomed like a woman!' I didn't get it. I guessed this Curtis guy and Reggie's father, Johnny Dionne, were about the same age. I didn't understand French, and still thought a fag was a cigarette. But Reggie got it, and he shouted loud, "Hey, Curt . . . Fuck off!" and the room fell silent. Uncles George and Paul caught Reggie's arm before he got his swing in on this asshole named Curtis, and they ushered Reggie and Curt outside to cool off.

I was looking for action out the front window. It was dark, but shadows were provided by the moon on the snow. I could see what appeared to be the back of my Uncle George, and it looked like he was peeing on the driver's door of my Dad's Mercury Cougar.

I said, "Dad . . . I do believe Uncle George is whizzing on your car." Aunt Bernice opened up the front door, letting a chill in and heat out as she said, "George, shame on you. Behave yourself."

When Reggie came back inside, we all cheered and said, "Hey, Curt, Fuck off!"

He laughed, and shook his head, and said, "Who invited that guy, anyway?"

Most of us were spending the night at a motel out on the highway. I rode back with a responsible driver. We toured down the Delamere Road and through the village of Alban with our new driver, Jeannette. She had recently got her license; and her brother Chris, Mom, Dad, and me arrived safely to our beds. When I got out of the car, I stargazed for a bit where the big sky remains undisturbed. The constellations stood out brilliantly and appeared to be closer to earth.

When I asked Uncle George, "Why did you pee on our car?" His answer was a smug grin and "Hee, hee, hee," that I'll never forget. Then Aunt Bernice "Tisked, tisked," and at dawn we were calling it a night.

I was with my friends Karen and Laurie when we bumped into Bryan Cauldin at the Upper Canada Mall in New-market. He had his Doberman, Cisco, on a leash, wearing a muzzle and spiked collar for effect. We had gone to Newmarket by bus, but Bryan offered us a ride back in his mother's car. Laurie and Karen were nervous around his black and tan, so Bryan sat in the back in the middle with Cisco's head out the window on the left side and Laurie on his right. I was still a rookie driver, but I drove with Karen, my passenger, up front. It was a stupid arrangement, and not shocking that we got T-boned at the intersection of Aurora Side Road and Woodbine about four-thirty that afternoon.

We could have been killed. Mrs. Cauldin's car was a write-off. My Father was furious. My Mother was glad nobody got hurt. When my ticket and court summons arrived, it was ad-dressed to Pauline Kuerly. So we went to court and they called Pauline Kuerly, and it sounded like Curly . . . I stood up and said, "I'm not Pauline Curly, but I am Pauline Kiely". The Judge said, "Case dismissed." What? We beat the ticket. Somebody still had to pay for the tough old car that I totalled. Bryan was saying go, and Karen was saying no. Her glasses had snapped in half on impact, and my knees were all black and blue from hitting the steering column. I overheard my parents and the Cauldin's talk-ing about their deceased car, and something was said about sev-en hundred and fifty bucks. I was in my last year of High School and I worked part-time at the Stouffville Restaurant. We lived so far away that my job made no sense by the time Mom had to pick me up after school, and drive me in to Stouffville on Satur-days.

After that, the tension between me and Dad was tighter than a duck's arse, and that's water tight. Whenever I went out, he blew a gasket when I came in. I couldn't be trusted with the car or anything apparently. We had a huge argument, and I left home. I caught a ride with a friend from school to my friend Janet's place in Aurora. She lived in a townhouse with three other girls. For the first couple of days at the townhouse when everyone was gone to work, I would play my Jethro Tull or Janet's Queen album loud.

I had been coming home late because I had met a guy through Janet and her boyfriend Ron Connor. They had requested a guest pass for him to the Max Webster Concert at my school. This buddy of Connor's, whose name I had forgotten, got out of their car. He reminded me of Paul McCartney. He had almond shaped eyes and the longest eyelashes I'd ever seen. It was like a little bell went off in my head. I swear an angel whispered, "There's the father of your children."

When we were introduced he offered me the roach they'd been smoking in the car. That night I forgot I was there with my boyfriend of six months, Mike Cassidy. Because I had forgotten this guy's name when I signed him up on the guest sheet, I had pencilled in Charlie Pride. Brad Parsons wasn't impressed. The show was great, and then Janet, Ron, and Brad followed me and Mike back to my house for a night cap. My parents knew most of my friends, and Mom made coffee and sandwiches, and Dad offered people a beer. He was surprised to learn that Connor never touched alcohol. His old man had been a good for nothing drunk, and he had no use for the stuff.

At the end of the evening my Father says to Mike Cassidy, "Mikey, my boy, I get the feeling it's been nice knowing you. It would appear my daughter's affections have turned." It was harsh, but true, and that obvious. Brad and I made plans to go roller skating the next day at The Terrace downtown, and were an item after that.

His mother was a widow with four kids, and his family lived in an apartment at Jane and Finch, a tough part of town where there were racial gang fights, drugs, and crime. There were chicken bones in the ashtray in the lobby at 4800 Jane, and urine in one corner of the elevator. His mother was out-of-place in this community. She was a good looking red-head with strong morals and values. She was working on a way out of 'The Jungle.' Mrs. Parsons regularly went bowling with a bitter, elderly farmer that apparently had a big house in the country to go with his big bank roll. When I met Brad's family, my heart went out to them, especially his ten-year-old sister Brenda.

My Father said he worried sick over his daughter alone in the big city. I got a job through Karen and Laurie in the mailroom at Tomenson, Saunders, and Whitehead Insurance Brokers in the Toronto Dominion Centre. Morning and evening I travelled up and down Yonge Street in a brown van with this guy from the townhouse next door who worked as a Courier.

Jeannette was a typist for The Permanent Trust Company, and Denise was working for the Post Office. Jeannette had the idea that Denise, I, and she should rent an apartment at Graydon Hall. So we did. The price was right and the place was nice enough, but the location between Shepherd and York Mills on Don Mills was the pits for public transit.

Our apartment was on the twenty-third floor. It had three bedrooms and two bathrooms, and cost three hundred and seventy-seven dollars split three ways a month. Brad slept over a couple of times a week. Janet moved in with us, but she and Ron quit their jobs to stay home and make love and a mess all day; so we had to ask them to leave.

I went alone across town by bus to an East Indian female doctor seeking birth control. I had the prescription filled and was all set as soon as I got my period, as much as I hoped and prayed it didn't come. I was out from under my parent's rules and roof for three months, and I'd always said that if this happened to me I would go out west to the nuns and give the child up for adoption. It was a delicate predicament. It was February, and I wasn't eighteen until June. Brad had a friend who said that his sister had got knocked up and she went to a doctor who took care of it. I was so tired, and thought I may as well call my kid "I told you so", because that's what I'm going to hear for the rest of my life!" Fear and anxiety screamed louder than the voice of reason. I had an appointment with the infamous Dr. Morgentaler, and he took care of my problem.

When I woke from the anaesthetic that problem was gone, but I had a new one, a much worse one. I was racked in guilt, remorse, and shame. Denise met me and took me home. We travelled in silence. Brad was at our apartment, waiting. In an attempt to console me, he said, "That must be a huge relief." I replied, "Brad, every time I look in a stroller or see a child I will remember what I did today. I murdered someone, my own baby . I hate myself." I pleaded with God for forgiveness, but I couldn't forgive myself. I promised I would do my best to make things right. This would be my cross to carry, the black mark on my soul. I could never ever say anything bad about anyone else because I was the lowest of the low. I had done the unforgivable, committed a mortal sin. A song called *The Butcher Boy* played over and over in my head :

> *On Moore Street where I did dwell,*
> *a butcher boy I loved quite well,*
> *He courted me my life away,*
> *and now with me he will not stay.*
> *I wish my baby it was born,*
> *and smiling on its daddy's knee,*
> *But my wishes they will be dead and gone,*
> *as the long green grass is growing over me.*
> *He went upstairs and the door he broke,*
> *he found her hanging by a rope,*
> *He took his knife and he cut her down,*
> *and in her pocket these words he found.*
> *"Oh dig my grave large wide and deep,*
> *Place a marble stone at my head and feet,*
> *And in my middle a turtle dove,*
> *So the world will know that I died for love."*

Brad and I took in a triple bill of three horror flicks one afternoon. We saw *Tales from the Crypt, Texas Chain Saw Massacre,* and *The Exorcist* back to back. Even though I mostly looked at Brad's ear and covered my eyes, I was a mess as a result of the graphic images and surreal sound effects. I had bad dreams, and a hard time just closing my eyes long enough to wash my face.

Early Saturday morning on the July long weekend in 1979 Brad and I caught a ride with my cousin Chris in the back of his truck to the *Beaulieu Family Reunion* at Uncle Gill's. On account of work obligations at a little snack bar in Bruce's Mill, I had missed the first one the year before. I failed to see how rough camping in the wilderness would be such a great time, but Jeannette insisted it was 'awesome'. There was no way I was going to miss out on 'awesome'.

We weren't as lucky with the weather this year. The weekend was cold and wet. There was a good turn-out of about ninety with forty odd tents of all shapes, colours, and sizes, and a couple of campers in the big field. Conveniences included a sink, outhouses, bon-fire, and the lake which was about a fifteen minute walk from camp. This weather encouraged hungry mosquitoes which never let up, and discouraged swimming. The mozzies showed no mercy, even landing on the steaks on the BBQ. People huddled around the fire, and in the tents we talked, sang, and got caught up with each other.

Uncle Paul and his wife Jean had six children before their marriage ended: Darryl, Rae, Laura, Terry, Brenda and Rachel. Uncle Paul with his new woman, Nicolle, and his offspring Laura, Terry, and Brenda were campers this weekend. I sat next to my Uncle at the fire. He had white hair and warm brown eyes with full dark lashes, much the same as my Mother's. He said, "Nothing went to waste when we were kids. My mother had to count and ration everything. Nobody had much money in Alban. One time I am still very young, it was maybe 1945. Me and my brodder, John, and Johnny Dionne, we borrow this horse and this big box sleigh, and we go down to the saw-mill there in Bigwood. We are going for a load of pulp wood, the scraps for firewood for my mother. It is very cold, and we loaded up this boxed-in sleigh and were on our way back home when the sleigh, it gets caught and stuck on the train tracks down there by the Murdock river. Johnny Dionne was the man in charge. When we heard the train coming in the distance, my brodder, he run down the tracks thinking he could stand in the middle and wave his arms and get the train to stop . . . but it didn't, and he has to jump into the ditch. Just in time Johnny Dionne, he unhitched that horse and leads it to safety. The train it cut the wagon in half, and our load of wood it was smashed.

Alice Beaulieu with all her daughters - 1945

People in the village they hear the sound of this, so some come to see what has happened. I remember how pale Johnny

Dionne was, and how this horse it was shaking. It was a close call that time."

My Auntie Anne proudly wears her mother's wedding ring on her baby finger. It is a tall gold band that was blessed and placed on the third left finger of Alice Rancourt when she said, "I do." to Eugene Beaulieu on May 6, 1924.

"This was the start of the family," Aunt Anne said, "Apparently they lived with his parents, while their house at the farm was being built. My mother prayed the rosary every day, and asked God to keep us together. After my father died, she easily could have given up and put us up for adoption, but she didn't. Instead she took in the Marchand girls, and did her best. We had nothing. Your mother and I would find sticks and say they were our dolls, and your mother would dance to the bell on the alarm clock. My mother's only prayer that we would stay together has come true, and I think she would be happy and proud today. Maybe she is here with us. It is funny to be back in Alban. It all seems so long ago."

Jacquie Marchand said, "Memère was worn out by the time it came to us. By the time I was a teenager, she had it. She didn't talk much anymore, and she was quick with her fly swatter or the back of her hand." Jacquie fondly remembered when Uncle Oscar was in the army, and he sent home twelve gold Christmas tree balls. "Memère never said anything, but she would stare at those balls and that tree."

There were three generations around this campfire, the little ones toasting marshmallows and waving the smoke out of their faces. "When you think about all of us in that little shack, poor Mom, and then the cousins would come in and play cards." Uncle Oscar said.

"Well, it wasn't like we were allowed out after dark. That's why they came to our house." Auntie Agnes added, "On Saturday nights we'd have cards going at the kitchen table, and a bunch listening to the hockey game on the radio in the other room."

My Mother said, "Do you remember those hockey games with *Rocket Richard* and *Gordie Howe*? The house was never dull. Do you remember the way Mom couldn't afford the license to listen to the radio so she kept it hidden under the bed, and we could only listen to it for a half hour?"

The Beaulieu Family Reunion was Uncle Gabe and Aunt Olga's brainstorm. They even had games for kids and adults that they called "Beau-lympics" on Sunday afternoon. Even though the weather wasn't playing nice, we sure had a good time. When My Mom was singing French songs around the fire with her sisters, Agnes, Doloris, Anne, Bette, and her nieces, Jacquie, Alice, and Celine, they sure looked and sounded like a bunch of squaws. The fire danced to their chanting, and they were all tanned, with dark hair and eyes, and high cheek bones.

My Mother sang:

> *"I'm an Indian big and strong,*
> *I go hunting all day long.*
> *Bows and arrows are my toys.*
> *I go hunting with the boys."*

Over the years: family New Year's parties, reunions, weddings, showers, anniversaries, and special-occasion birthdays. We made the effort. We got together, and stayed in touch. I never forgot the story that my Mother said she heard from her mother:

> *A Cherokee elder was teaching his grandchildren about the meaning of life.*
> *He said to them, "There is a fight going on inside of me. It is a terrible fight and it is between two wolves.*
> *One wolf is evil. He is fear, anger, envy, sorrow, regret, greed, arrogance, self-pity, resentment, inferiority, lies, false pride, competition, superiority and ego.*

The other wolf is good. He is joy, peace, love, hope, sharing, serenity, humility, kindness, benevolence, friendship, empathy, generosity, truth, compassion and faith.

"This same fight is going on inside all of you. In fact it is going on inside everyone on earth."

The children thought about this for a very long time and then one child asked his grandfather, "Which wolf will win?"

The old Cherokee simply replied, "The one you feed."

Chapter Twelve

The Funny Farm

We had many parties and good times at the apartment in Graydon Hall. There never was much in the way of food. For Denise, Jeannette, and I, life was a diet. We crunched on Triscuit crackers for breakfast and feasted for pennies a day on the staple, Kraft Dinner (macaroni and cheese). Once we went grocery shopping after smoking a joint, and we drank chocolate milk, made sandwiches and ate them right in the store. We put a decent dent in a bag of cookies, but paid full price for this half-eaten bag. This was the late seventies.

Denise drove a motor bike, *a chick bike,* she said. It was a Honda 450. When she got caught in the rain on the 401 highway in a t-shirt, she came in really pissed off, saying "You'd think people never saw a set of knockers before." Then she slammed the door to her room.

Denise was cute in her postal carrier uniform for the City of Toronto, especially in the summer time wearing shorts. There were warnings on the radio about some eclipse, that if you looked at it you'd go blind. Denise had nightmares, and got insomnia, and she was angry about that too. It was rare that gentle Denise ever raised her voice, but she was shouting, "It's like I finally fall to sleep, and I dream about these kids playing in a school yard, and then they see me, and they're pointing 'Postie,

Postie, look at the eclipse, look at the eclipse', and then they're all looking at it, and I know they're going blind."

My Ballantrae friends didn't have cars, but Ruth was pretty steady with Jay Thomas who had wheeled a deal with Ferdi on a pink 1966 Policeman Special Harley Davidson. Ferdi also helped Joey Smith piece together a Sportster, so the three of them bundled up and came for a visit to Graydon Hall occasionally. I don't know if they were vibrating from the ride or the cold. Joey would have a paper lunch bag half-full of home-grown, and we'd do our best to smoke it. Joey says to Denise, "You're a letter carrier, right?"

And she says, "Yep."

"My Income Tax Return is late. Maybe you can have a look around for it?"

I roared laughing, after a flash image of our little Denise in her uniform on a huge pile of mail scouring envelopes hoping to find *the one* addressed to Joe Smith.

Jay's father hailed from Belfast, so my Dad said I had to keep an eye on him. Jay was laying carpet during the day, and bouncing part-time at a bar in Markham called The Sherwood. This bar was about half way for both of us; so we'd try to hook up there for some of the better venues like Teenage Head. Brad was pretty quiet around my biker buddies from The Lake. He preferred the company of his friends and his brother Ben who was born a year less a day after Brad. Brad said they weren't really close. He was into music, and Ben was into hockey and sports.

Brad and I went to so many concerts. We saw Queen, ZZ Top, and Ted Nugent at Maple Leaf Gardens; Johnny Winter, The Ramones, Meatloaf, and ELO at the CNE. We were front row for The Clash at The O'Keefe Centre. In the summer there would be concerts at Ontario Place where we'd catch Murray McLaughlin, Burton Cummings, or our folk favourite, John Prine. Brad was a city boy. He was happiest at *Sam the Record Man*. We became groupies for the bar band, GODDO, featuring Greg Godovitch, Gino Scarpelli, and a handsome drummer that only looked left or right. How come it's the cute guy who doesn't make eye contact? If they were playing the Piccadilly Tube, me and Brad, and whoever we could muster up, were front row.

One night a bouncer grabbed me from behind when I came out of the washroom. He rubbed himself up against my back, felt me up and said, "You're hot." I could feel the heat of his bad breath on my neck. It was nasty. When he let go of me, I told Brad who could tell I was shook up about something when I returned to our table.

Later that night a group of bouncers grabbed Brad, roughed him up in the hallway, and then threw him out. Brad walked out onto Yonge Street and kicked over an innocent chestnut cart in rage. By the time I realized he was missing and went outside, there was an older man waving his arms over his toppled business, chestnuts scrambled over Yonge Street, and a Policeman putting cuffs on Brad who was against his car with his hands behind his back. I pleaded with the cop to let me take Brad home, and I opened the back door for him to get out of the cruiser. But the police officer assured me that if I continued to interfere, I too would be spending the night in the *grey bar hotel.*

Brad spent that night in the 52 Division drunk-tank. He went home to his mother's early the following morning. I had gone back to the apartment with a few stragglers. When I didn't hear from Brad by noon the next day, I called Mrs. Parsons. He was home and we made arrangements to get together later. A mutual friend, Ian, who was still hanging around hung-over from the night before was heading in the same direction. We decided to ride the bus together. Ian was a nice guy, good-looking too. He came in to a church, and lit a candle with me when I asked if we could stop to say a prayer.

On the May 24 weekend Ian drowned in a canoe accident. I was devastated. I had never had anyone my own age that I personally knew die before. Sure my Grandmother and Grandfather, but I had been young and considered them old. I consoled myself thinking that at their ripe old ages they were probably ready to check out! Given my hysterics, Brad felt it best if I didn't attend Ian Young's funeral as I didn't really know him as well as most of the others. I was convinced that God was punishing me for *the secret.*

Denise was in an on-again-off again relationship with a guy named Dale who rented a townhouse in Brampton with Wally and my friend Janet's boyfriend, Ron. Denise and Dale both had bikes and enjoyed camping. Jeannette had started seeing a guy from Claremont, some guy her father knew from Semple and Gooder whose name was Rick Timms. It turned out Brad's father had worked with his uncle, and that they had played together as kids. Rick figured it out because Brad looked so much like his father, and Rick remembered seeing Mr. Parsons at his Uncle's without his wife and family sometimes. Mrs. Parsons said, "There had been a bus strike when my husband passed away, and Rick's Uncle picked us up from the hospital." Sadly her husband had passed away right in front of his wife and children after removing his oxygen mask to speak with them.

At Christmas time Janet and I went shopping at Yorkdale Mall. I tried on this coat, a black leather coat with a fur collar. It had a price tag of one hundred and forty- nine dollars. On Christmas Eve I gave Brad a Jew's harp, sort of a trinket, because he liked music so much. He'd bought me the leather coat, and I starved myself to stay thin and wear it. I shared all my fears with Brad, and he let me draw tattoos on him. I was sure we were destined for each other. We made love.

Brad embraced the family, and we would host even bigger parties at the apartment with his friends and my cousins. He fit in at the family reunion, and got along great with Colleen, Sean, and Jim. We took my brothers to the Toronto Zoo, and a couple of movies in the city. They were more amused and interested in riding the subway.

Rick and Jeannette were always together. They hardly ever did part. They spent a lot of time talking and giggling in her room, and went for candlelight dinners alone. I was seriously jealous when Jeannette got engaged only seven months after dating Rick. I mean really! I was almost twenty, and Brad and I had been going together for over two years. I was pretty much an old maid according to Granny Clampett from *The Beverly Hillbillies.*

Pauline Kiely, Jeannette and Denise Beaulieu - 1978

After a brief engagement, they got married in Rexdale in October. Uncles Ross and Oscar had to miss moose hunting; so they put on their orange vests and hunting caps in protest during speeches. Everyone tapped their wineglasses for Jeannette and Rick to kiss so many times that Jeannette started saying, "Mom and Dad, you kiss." or "Pauline and Rod, you kiss." Rod, tall, awkward, and seventeen was Rick's kid brother, and my partner for this wedding. Rick's other brother, Randy, had died in a tragic motorcycle accident. Before Rod kissed me, the bugger dips me backwards and whispers in my ear, "You're marrying the wrong guy. I'm in love with you." Then he plants this big 'Rhett-Butler-in-Gone-with-the-Wind-kind-of-kiss' on me. I was taken aback, and pushed him away, saying, "I'm engaged."

Brad stood up and said, "Listen, cowboy, I've got a bow and arrow under the table."

My Father laughed, and shook Roy's hand, Rick's father, and said, "That kid's got brass balls."

Rick's mother, Rosemary, sang with the voice of an angel during the service.

Jeannette moved in with Rick, and Denise moved in with Dale. Brad got a basement apartment in Willowdale, and I bought a brand new Dodge Omni sports car, and moved back home. I was saving for our wedding, and had only been commuting two months when my Father dropped the bomb.

One muddy Sunday in March he asked me to go for a drive. We headed north-east a good twenty minutes. He turned into a long driveway on a dilapidated ruin of a farm. It was directly north of the windy hamlet of Zephyr. Dad said, "What do you think, Paul? I've got a firm offer in on it."

"God, you are joking. Right?" I replied.

My heart sank into my guts because Brad and I had been planning our wedding for September. Part of that wedding vision included cocktails and summer parties at the house. Our nice house. The one I'd helped them build. "Dear God, no," my blood screamed as I looked around at what resembled very much the set for the TV sit-com *Green Acres,* starring Eddie Arnold and Eva Gabor. But this wasn't acting. This was really happening. He looked so chuffed with himself while I wanted to puke. "Seriously, Dad, you mean it. You have bought this place. Seriously. It's a fucking mess. Look around you. All I see is mud."

He had that big smile and said, "Pauline, let's take a walk!"

I.R.A. protestor Bobby Sands was on a hunger strike. He lasted sixty-six days before he died for the cause. I debated on going on a hunger strike as we walked through this empty old house. There was a big old Findlay oven in the centre of the kitchen. The floors were linoleum with paths worn through. Plastic curtains were gently moving even though the windows were closed. The wainscoting was dark and the plaster ceilings

were high. Cobwebs hung everywhere and upstairs everything
was painted what he called "farmer green". It must have been on
sale because this sad green was the only contrast on the cupboards, cabinets, doors, and door frames. There was even an
outhouse, and the wreck of a chicken coop that had seen better
centuries. His story was that the previous owners had grown old
with no heirs. There was a hundred and forty-seven acres, but
the house was to be desired. It had sat empty for the better part
of two years. Dad said, "This old place is on life support and will
need a full overhaul, including an oil change. Who's better for
the job? I got it for a song, a-hundred-and-fifty grand." He let me
know we would be moving in this June. Brad and I had mailed
out overseas invitations early for our wedding in September. My
eyes were open, but I couldn't see what my Father saw.

Maureen and Harry were coming from England with Declan and Sadie. Dave and Kate were separated now, but Kate,
Tina, and Greg wouldn't miss it for the world, as well as Moira
and Rory, with their three: Stan, Trixie, and Will. "Where will
we put them all?" my Mother fretted. She said, "I'll put my
shoulder to the wheel one more time for you, John Kiely. I think
you're crazy, but you haven't steered me wrong so far." And she
dug in and cleaned, and painted, and sanded, and scraped wall
paper, and hung wall paper, and created a beautiful home for us
just in time. Everyone had worked hard all summer, but it was
Mom at ninety pounds who appeared to be the most worn out.
The carpet-layers were kicking in the broadloom when my Father went to the airport to pick up the first batch of arrivals.
When Uncle Harry walked in he called me Yolande. Moira and
Rory's crew were young. Trixie was seven, and she still had her
blanket that she called her tickle. Except for meals we hardly
saw Stan and Will, or Sean and Jim.

Maureen and Harry would spend a few days at *The Farm,*
but they would spend most of their visit with their son, Thomas,
and his new wife Crystal who had immigrated to Canada the
year prior. Thomas was a pastry chef who had been hired by
Truffles Restaurant at The Four Seasons Hotel. He had served

the Queen Mum at Lloyds of London back in England during cul-
inary college.

Moira said, "When we were kids there was a photograph
of Uncle Joe on the mantle at Aunt Peggy's, my Mammy's only
full sister. Mammy had step-sisters, but this picture of her true
brother, Joseph Johnston, was a mystery. The man had survived
the TB, and run off and joined the British Army. Aunt Peggy
told us Joe became a civil engineer. Everyone that came through
the door were shown this photo, and introduced to the infamous
Uncle Joe, his wife Doris, and their children, Barry, Janet, and
Glynn, in Arabia." One night around Christmas we were at home
around the fire; and out of the dark and pouring rain, a knock
comes to our door. I opened it, and there were these people bundled up in coats, standing there getting wet. For a bit of crack, I
said, 'It must be Uncle Joe, home from Arabia, and this your
wife, Doris, and the children, Barry, Janet, and Glynn.' And
from under the brim of his fedora says he, 'I am. It t'is. How did
you know? And who might you be?' I nearly shit meself."

Aunt Kate said, "Your Da and I were professional mourners. When somebody died in the neighbourhood the family would
put a black ribbon on their door. The immediate family members
also wore a black ribbon band on their arm to show that they
were in mourning. They'd have the body laid out in the sitting
room of their house, and anyone could go in and say a prayer. So
there'd John and I be snickering through a prayer for some
stranger in hopes of a fizzy drink, a fancy sambo, or a sweet."

The Farm still didn't make a good first impression. The
grounds and outside of the house were tidied up over the summer, but the out buildings were still dilapidated. There was a
drive shed, a log cabin, a big dirty dairy barn, and that nasty,
filthy, chicken coop. Pixie had passed away. At fifteen the little
pasta eater got tired, and trotted off one day and never returned.
So we only had the black mutt from the pound called Tramp,
Super-Tramp to Colleen. This new dog had eaten one of Sean's
balloons and puked it up in the car. My Father had told my

Mother that he'd thought his kids were getting soft, sort of spoiled in the other house. He felt his boys needed more space.

A friend of Gail Tripp's had given my folks her old horse, Lady, to retire. Lady was twenty. She would be company for Kella. These two horses and a few head of cattle were grazing at *The Farm* on moving day. Wee Lass had given birth to Bonnie Wee Lass, and the place looked a bit brighter as the grass was green and the apple blossoms were in bloom in the old orchard. Jay loved the place. He said it felt haunted. Ruth agreed with me and my Mother that really my Father should have his head tested.

Dad's friends from the Mount Albert Lion's Club, Harvey and Ted, would be bartending at the wedding. They were bobbing their heads and smiling as they looked around. The view was fantastic. The house and barn were on a very high point. Down in the valley was the orchard, a field, then a train track, and the Egypt Sideroad. Straight out you could challenge your eyes to see as far as they could focus. Rolling green hills dotted with barns, fence rows, and tree tops. When all the bottles of my Mother's homemade wine broke in the shed, she thought they may have had frost or something. Auntie Agnes insisted it was because of the rumble of the train through the ground.

Two queen beds and two twin beds had been set up in the large master bedroom. Those first few nights we could hear the mice scurrying under us and up the walls. We got a couple of cats, and the next few nights we laughed in the dark at the sounds of the cats chasing mice. My Father said, "Good night, Pollyanna, good night Sean-boy; good night, Colleen Joy; and good night, Jim-bob." My Mother said, "We are the crazy Kielys!" and covered her head.

Our wedding gifts were so very generous. The four families had pooled their money and bought us a television. Brad and I could have romantic dinners on our Royal Albert 'Old Country Roses' china. We received silver candelabras, and Waterford Crystal. Even one of my Father's customers extended her well wishes in the token form of a solid brass swan. Prince Charles and Lady Diana had their Royal Wedding on July 29th, and we followed suit with our Royal Wedding Sept 26, 1981. During my Father's speech, he said, "I don't know what this guy's got, but my daughter thinks the sun shines out his backside."

Pauline Kiely - 1981

Brad and I spent our honeymoon at The Briar's Inn in Jackson's Point. We did what newlyweds do for a couple of days. I had booked a room in the old part and our four poster bed had feather pillows and a down duvet. Brad's allergies were bad. His breathing was laboured. I enjoyed some champagne and a long soak in the deep clawfoot tub.

When we arrived back at *The Farm*, things were in full swing for at least another week. It was a wet summer, and the beefsteak tomatoes in the garden were enormous. We would car pool and convoy for day trips to Niagara Falls, The Science Centre, or The Eaton Center; and then come home to burgers, a roast, or turkey that my Mother had fussed over all day. She said she preferred to stay back, tidy up, and stock up for the next shift in the kitchen. If we ate out, it was generally Kentucky Fried Chicken because Sadie and Rory couldn't get enough of the Colonel's secret recipe.

Uncle George and Aunt Bernice celebrated twenty-five years of marriage; and shortly after that, Jeannette found out she was having a baby. Shortly after that, Uncle George got sick. He turned pale, and lost weight. It was cancer, asbestos cancer. Thank God, Jeannette had Rick. I did my best, but was awful at this stuff. And this was so close, so heartbreaking. Uncle George disappeared before our eyes. He left us on November 22, 1982, and shortly after we lost Uncle John, and then Uncle Paul on February 4, 1984.

My Mother said, "Thank God, there isn't a Ringo."

For the most part we had shared happy times at showers, jack and jill's, and weddings. Then bam, we get hit with a string of funerals, each so painful it took a piece of us. At Uncle John Beaulieu's funeral, my Dad was driving his new used Brougham Cadillac. It was a big brown car, full of buttons, and my Mother powered her window down as the Caddy hearse drove past. She says to Marcel who was walking by, "We decided to ride in one while we are still alive."

Sometimes I forget that she is a French girl from Alban who was taught to speak English by an Irishman, the guy who had said, "You've got a mouth in your head; so use it." Sometimes her words sound harsher than she means. "Mom, that's terrible." I said.

She said, "My brother Johnny could always take a joke." And she reminded me that this was her brother, and that she knew the man. I was kind of humbled because she actually paid him a bit of a tribute by reminding us how he loved to laugh. Then my Mother starts humming and eventually singing, *Another One Bites the Dust* before her window slowly goes up. Marcel is, of course, laughing at his crazy Aunt Yolande. I love his dimples.

This was her brother, with similar colouring and features to her own: Johnny Beaulieu with whom they had partied in

Montreal with B.C., before children; John Beaulieu who called my old man "O'Malley"; the mischievous character, who had married Frieda, a cousin of Bernice, from Marmora; Brother John who stuck his tongue on the door knob when they were kids, and when Memère pulled the door open to see what all the noise was about, she also pulled a layer of skin off of his tongue, so he got to eat popsicles and have special treatment; Pat, Brian, and Rickie's dad who got emphysema and it got worse. Here's how he said goodbye. "When I die, I want them to cremate my body, and then spread my ashes around up north at Gill's there. Every time you see a dandelion you can think of me."

When we got a little lost on the way home, my Father said, "We're the fuckawie tribe."

I said, "What?"

He said, "Where the fuck are we?"

My cousin Terry, Uncle Paul's son, said, "Dad and I were just stacking some firewood, and he put his hand to his chest and couldn't catch his breath, and he was gone. It was that fast."

The Uncle Paul I knew was a gentle, peaceful man. Apparently years ago, there had been another Uncle Paul who drank too much and grew depressed and angry. My Uncle Paul had been sober for more than twenty years.

Brad and I chummed around with Gary Keough and his new girlfriend, Janice Evanoff. We had people come and go in the crowd, but for the most part it was a solid bunch. Saturday nights during the winter the guys who referred to themselves as 'the boys from Driftwood' played a cheap hour of shinny hockey at Double Rink's Arena. We girls took up a table having cocktails and a few laughs in the bar called *The Penalty Box*.

Brad, Janice, and I went for a two-day drive with Gary in his black Dodge Duster to P.E.I. That's where the Keough's hail from. In fact as soon as we stepped off the ferry in Summerside, his "Pappy" as he called him was right there. This old guy was the first local I saw sitting in a lawn chair. Gary says to the old man, "Pappy, it's me, Gary, Joe's boy from Toronto. Where's Mammie?"

"Here comes the eigit now." the old geezer replies, as he's shaking Gary's hand. While Gary is telling Pappy our names, I see his grandmother coming up the street, spry with a basket of raspberries. She picked up her step and waved because she recognized her grandson.

We listened to *Dr. Hook* and *Bad Company* cassette tapes over and over. We drank Alpine beers and smoked honey oil, black hash, and a bit of weed. The sand and soil were red, and we had to pick our way through jelly fish on the beach. Gary's family were really hospitable. We played tourist, ate our fill of lobster and fresh baked cinnamon buns.

Gary asked Brad to be his best man, and Janice asked me to be her maid-of-honour. He ate a dozen goldfish at his stag to raise money. The only problem was I would be due to have a baby around the time she was planning their wedding. My talented mother and her Singer sewing machine managed to create a burgundy ensemble that served the purpose. My face looked like a full moon under the pill box hat.

I delivered a baby girl, six pounds and six ounces, ten days after the Keough's wedding. We named her Lacey Beth Parsons. Grandparents' hour was between four and five, and this was the first and only time in my life that I can remember my parents being a half-hour early. Of course they let them in. My Mother said, "We hardly slept a wink last night, Pauline. We talked about when you were born, and now here you are making us grandparents. I mean I like the idea of being a Memère, but I'm not sure about sleeping with Grandpa."

My Father held Lacey, and said, "I think she looks like a little Parsons." The room was filled with the smell of her and the little girl named Madison behind the curtain. Lacey was tiny. I used to call her "Chicken Legs." She had dark hair and dark blue eyes. I knew when it was she crying in the nursery, and never left her there very long. Lacey was our precious little dolly that came home from the hospital in the canary yellow '55 Chevy Pick-up, this big old steel tank that had no power steering and windshield wipers that heaved themselves back and forth with great effort. It was a good thing for Brad that I had learned to drive standard.

The 1955 Chevy Pick-up

My family had all gone to Ireland for four weeks. Dad and the boys would be doing some repairs to Granny's house. I missed them. We did our best to do the chores at *The Farm* on weekends. A local lad named Perry Mason fed the animals during the week, but they missed the family too. The last week was the longest.

Brad and I drove the Caddy to the airport to pick them up. My sister who had left this country looking beautiful returned to us, 'looking like something the cat dragged in,' as my Mother would say. Colleen had been out at an all-night party with Mick and Tess. She walked past me in a daze and said, "Paul, I had the best time."

Then Dad came through those airport doors that zip open and said, "Wait till you see what I brought you." I was holding Lacey when the doors zipped open again. There was my Mother with Granny in tow, linked to her arm. Sean popped out from behind them, snickering. Tears just flowed from my eyes, and I passed the baby to Brad. I greeted my Granny and I hugged her, and says she to my Mother, "Told you there'd be a scene."

It was late March with remnants of winter in the form of white patches of crusty snow along the 401 highway, and my grandmother asked, "What's that?"

So I said, "It's what's left of the snow."

And says she, "Wouldn't you t'ink the road crew would be out there with packages of salt to be done with it?" For a brief moment I entertained the mental image of road crews all over the country with packages of salt.

Jim hung on to the baby, and Brad drove home because my Father said he was still on Irish time.

4 Generations, Pauline, John, Granny, and Lacey - 1984

Chapter Thirteen

The Bee's Knees

Mom and Dad didn't have much coaxing to do to get Granny to fly back with them to meet her first great-granddaughter, baby Lacey. Granny was calling herself, "Jet-set Lizzy." It was easy to tug on her heart strings because she would also get to see Theresa, Brenna and Dan, Alicia and Jacob, Thomas and Crystal, and our newest Canadian, Sadie. Two of Maureen and Harry's flock had flown the coup for Canada. They were thankful Declan was still at home as he was in love with Susie. Sadie said her brother's girlfriend was a snake charmer because she had inherited a python named Fred.

I'd felt the first twinges of labour when I woke up in the morning, but had no real pain or anything until around eleven that night, right after my favourite soap, *Dynasty*. I said, "Brad, we better go to the hospital now."

Brad and I climbed into "Old Yeller," and arrived at York Central Hospital in Richmond Hill where they proceeded to break my water. Then nature took its course; and after two pushes at two-thirty on October 6th, there she was. New to this world, Lacey wasn't crying; she was just peeping all around with those big eyes. She had black hair that stood up and Brad said,

"She looks like Dr. Woo." My body shook from the shock, but the nurses comforted me with warm blankets. Lacey was our little dolly in her tiny socks and frilly knickers. She'd be all bundled up sleeping peacefully in the *Jenny Lind* cradle Denise had lent me.

The year before, the annual *Beaulieu Family Reunion* had been switched to the August long weekend, and it was there in 1980 that I remember when Auntie Agnes got the call on the new telephone line Uncle Gill had installed. Patsy had had the baby.

"It's a girl! It's a girl! I'm a Memère! I'm a Memère! My scrawny Auntie Agnes yelled as she was running and jumping, coming from the house to the campsite. Patsy had married John Hudson, and now they had Carrie Anne.

Denise chose to skip all the wedding hoop-la because she was content in her relationship with Marty. While I was busy planning a wedding, they had been busy waiting on the arrival of Keith, the little angel that lit up our world on Christmas Day of 1981. He was born in Women's College Hospital so Jeannette and I went there to meet him on Boxing Day. I remember his ruby red full lips and Denise's perfect miniature features.

It was a new wave of babies, produced by the cousins. Gail came through with "The Osso Twins." On a frosty February day the blonde identical twin brothers, Zac and Jeff, arrived via C-section at York Central Hospital. The cards in their plastic bassinets read Osso-1 and Osso-2; and these boys were Osso impossible to tell apart with the exception of a mole near Jeffrey's ear. Gail's body suffered greatly during the pregnancy. She was hospitalized twice with kidney stones. These boys were big ones, nearly seven pounds each, thanks to their Estonian daddy, Eric, who is six-five.

Jeannette and all her family were just thrilled by the arrival of "Sweet Marie" in March. Rick's mother, after never having had a girl, just relished sharing her brag book with the ladies from the church choir. Auntie Bernice had a soft spot for babies. She and Uncle George had cared for many foster infants from The Children's Aid Society for many years. Seeing as he was out of town a lot, Auntie B did most of the caring; but we all knew that when he was home Uncle George had a genuine love for the little ones. Copper-haired Marie Claire was like a breath of fresh air.

I didn't see Ginette much those days but I had heard she had married Mike Nordover, and that they had a son, Lucas. I only saw Luke once when he was a baby. Patsy had a second daughter she named Candace the August before I had Lacey. Brad and I were living in a basement apartment on Bluegrass Boulevard in Richmond Hill across the street from Pat and John at this time.

Brad and I spent a lot of time at *The Farm* the summer I was expecting. It was always all hands on deck as there was no shortage of projects My Old Man had on the go. Shortly after the company went home after our wedding, my Father drove his bulldozer into the side of the house. We were having breakfast when he tore off the summer kitchen. Then he came inside with that big grin shouting, "Let there be light." Brad was allergic to almost everything: dust, grass, and fur; and he was stubborn about taking medication for it. He sneezed and wheezed; so we kept him out of the barn. Over time in the great outdoors his allergies got better.

Just before I had Lacey we were out for a walk on *The Farm* and noticed a nice house for sale in the little hamlet of Cedarbrae which was basically a dozen or so houses of various shapes and sizes placed along a concession road near a railway crossing. I was curious as to how much this house would cost. With the baby coming, we'd be outgrowing our basement apartment. I didn't really know how to look after a baby, and I wasn't comfortable with leaving her with a stranger.

The couple that owned the house weren't home. Their neighbour told us, "They have horses, and are building on ten acres on Stoney Batter Road". This neighbour, Otto, introduced his wife as Marsha, but he called her "Mini". She wore her highlighted hair short. She had twinkling green eyes, fine features, and was the first person I had ever met that wore a ring on her toe. She said that little ring drew a lot of attention, and that she was also expecting their first child in December.

The hundred and forty-seven acres of land was what sold my Father. He said, "I can always fix up or build a house." It was so serene in the hardwood forest with its tall straight maples, with the big patch of mature white birch at one end. We found a giant maple that Dad said would be the great-great-grandfather of this forest. The cedar and hemlock were also well established, much older than any of us.

As we walked along these trails I commented, "This looks like the kind of place where Winnie the Pooh and his friends would live." And from then on, that one particular trail in our forest was identified as 'Winnie the Pooh'.

There was an artesian well on the property where a gurgle of water sprang naturally from the ground out of the side of a hill. It gurgled year round. There was a long cedar log that was hollowed out like a trough strategically placed to transport the cool fresh water to the steel drum at its end for grazing livestock. There were walking or riding trails cut through the rented-out and planted fields of corn and soya. Dad leased out most of the workable land. He kept twenty-acres in hay to play farmer.

The Farm was a paradise for Colleen and me. We brought old Lady out of retirement and rode three nights a week, and rain-or-shine most Sunday afternoons until I was expecting. Lady was only fourteen hands high. I called her my little *Sportster* and rode her bareback. She was too old and small for Dad, but sometimes when he saw how much fun we were having, all two hundred and twenty pounds of him ended up on poor Kella's back. Kella was younger and stockier than Lady, but she would still huff and puff, and Colleen and I both said, "Dad, you need your own horse."

Colleen tried to coax Jim or Sean to go riding with her, but the boys were into power tools and making home movies with the new video camera.

The owners of the little white house got back to us. It had been on the market all summer, but honestly, no bites. We didn't have a lot of money, but had managed to save a few dollars. They wanted fifty-five thousand for this house. The lot was very small, but basically butted up to *The Farm*, so that was a bonus, not a bother. The trouble was the fact that the well was shared with two other houses; and one of these two houses also had a barn with running water. This raised our lawyer's eyebrows. We had to introduce ourselves to these potential new neighbours, and ask them to sign a statement saying they weren't experiencing any trouble with their water supply.

The first couple we had to approach were Kenny and Glady Green. She hailed from all of ten minutes away, Brown Hill. He was born and raised on a farm just over the hill east of this little hamlet in the fine Township of Georgina. Kenny was quite a character. He liked to mix Vodka with Kool-Aid. He called his concoction "California Kool-Aid!" Glady Green was a genuinely nice woman. Their son Buddy chummed with Jim, and Debbie Green was Sean's age. If she couldn't find her girl friends, she'd hang out with the boys.

The second door we knocked on was the residence of Lloyd and Dawn Tate. His Dad, Gordie, was a buddy of the infamous horse dealer, Dan Barkey. He regularly worked the auction sale ring at Toad Hall in Claremont. Lloyd drove a truck for Rainey Transport. These were the folks with the barn. Dawn had a couple of quarter horses, and was testing the market in goats. Lloyd fancied himself a cattle baron with a head of maybe fifteen or twenty Herefords.

Dawn said, "We're real close with his folks too."

"How did you guys meet?" I asked.

She said, "I was minding my own business waiting on tables at a Truck Stop down east, in Belleville, and this guy just kept coming in." Lloyd called his wife, Dawn - Barney, and his dog, Whip. When we asked the Tate's if they were having any trouble with the water, they told us about all sorts of troubles they were finding with their old place but water wasn't a problem. We were around the same age, and got into a few beers. When Lloyd said, "Barney can't cut me off 'cause she don't know where I'm gettin' it from." Brad laughed louder than I'd ever heard him before.

Papers were signed. We bought this house, and moved in Easter weekend. The day after we moved in, the well dried up. The bathroom and kitchen taps spat and coughed, and the toilets choked on mud. My Father came to the rescue. We soon had a drilled-well plus new gravel in the driveway. My Mother couldn't get enough of Lacey. She wasn't really sharing. The family would fight over who got to hold her and feed her. Jim was eleven when Lacey was born, and was even a good sport about changing her. Once he smeared peanut butter on a clean diaper, and then made a fuss when he took it off the baby. Jim smelled the diaper, and when he licked it we all freaked out.

The couple we bought the house from, Kim and Mike Warren, had left the place spotless. Given our long closing, Brad and I managed to save enough money for a new washer and dryer. We had the maple bedroom suite his mother and her friend had given us as a wedding gift, and enough bits and pieces to put together a nice little home.

I had nightmares and bad nerves when I took *the pill*; so we were using safes and tracking periods with the rhythm system. I found myself really very tired after the move, and knew I hadn't been keeping track of things; so I wasn't completely shocked to be expecting again.

This pregnancy was different, and this baby didn't flutter in my tummy. This one booted me in the bladder. For those around me this second pregnancy seemed to go by in no time, but for me, that last month was a suffering because it had been so very long since my body was my own.

The due date changed a couple of times before and after Christmas. We were all devastated when a snow-plow decapitated Mike Warren, and left his poor wife in the passenger seat without a scratch, or a husband, that January. My Mother always says, "A birth follows a death."

Finally I was induced at Newmarket Hospital late that January. Thanks to some pills and a drip on the twenty-fifth of the month, Leeann Jean Parsons was born, weighing in at seven pounds and fourteen ounces. Brad came into the delivery room outfitted in green scrubs and asked, "What can I do?"

I said, "Stretch your lips over your head and tell me how it feels."

Colleen popped by the hospital on her way to a party. She was all dolled up, took a look at the baby and said, "I think that baby looks like me, and you look like crap." I'd had a healthy baby sister for Lacey and a new little fairy for Grandpa to play with. LeeAnn was so sweet while I was nursing, but after four weeks we switched her over to formula and colic kicked in. Did this baby ever have colic. She cried, and cried, and cried, with tummy pains. I had to use suppositories to provide some relief. Turned out LeeAnn was lactose intolerant. When we switched her over to a soya-based diet, which in 1985 was still relatively new, she improved. My days were long, and I didn't really always know what to do with these babies. I remember our house being very clean, and always feeling so grateful to see my Mother, my lifeline, pull into our driveway in her little gold Chevette.

Although my family was only a country mile away, our farm being naturally divided by a railway line, was also on a dividing line for Bell Canada, so *The Farm* phone number was long distance. At thirty-four cents a minute, it made sense just to walk over.

The summer before, Colleen had asked a neighbouring farmer if she could pasture Kella with his stallion. The farmer had no problem with that, and my Father paid him in round bales of hay. When Colleen and Cameron were married, Kella gave her Bailey, the filly born just days after their wedding.

Almost the entire family was together on May 9th, 1987. Lacey was three, and she loved her little sister that she called "Wee Wee." LeeAnn had a good sense of humour once she was introduced to solid foods and wasn't so sick anymore.

The girls were the flower girls at my sister's wedding, and the Osso boys their partners as matching little ring bearers in tuxedos. As the event drew near my girls pleaded with my Mother, "Please no more pins, Memère." They were so tired of the alteration process of their pink and purple fancy dresses. The day arrived, and this wedding was one serious party. With the exception of Uncle Pat's clan, who for reasons I never understood wouldn't travel to Canada, pretty much everyone that had been invited arrived in style. A hundred and seventy representatives from Ireland, England, Sudbury, Alban, Fort Erie, St. Catherine's, Toronto, and the GTA.

The Farm was in good shape to host the two-to-three-week venue. Dad had put an addition on where he had torn the summer kitchen off; and now there was a large family room with a rusty-coloured brick fireplace. The Kiely crest hung proudly over the mantle, and on either side he had made maple cabinets with pot-lights in them where my Mother displayed our family heirlooms: a pewter bucking-bronco cowboy clock, some etched beer stein glasses, awards, trophies and trinkets that were gifts with sentimental value. Then there was the precious pear, a bottle of clear liquor that had a full size pear floating in it. 'The Pear' was said to have been very expensive, and we were all told it was "off limits". Taboo to touch 'The Pear'.

It was an open door policy, and there were six bedrooms plus a pull-out chesterfield. There was lots of parking at *The Farm*. You were welcome to bring your sleeping bags and curl up on the floor; but if you wanted some peace and privacy, you'd have to stay at the local motel.

Dad said, "This place is like an old whore; the more I give her, the more she takes."

I never smoked anything, or drank any alcohol during pregnancies; but after the babies were born, once in a while my Mother and I would have a chin-wag over some caffeine and nicotine. "A hooker's breakfast." is what she called this.

Dad had built what he called 'the monster deck'; and between him and his' dozer and tractors, the grounds were groomed and mostly all manicured now. The cherry tree was in blossom and tucked nicely out of the wind for pictures on my sister's big day.

Aunt Bette and Johnny Dionne had come to our house for a cup of tea the night before the wedding. I cut up rags, and bathed the girls so that Aunt Bette could set their long damp hair with the rags for ringlets. My Mother's oldest living sister told me that she remembers being small, like Lacey or LeeAnn, when her father lost his hat. She said, "We were all at the water because it was a hot day, but none of us were good swimmers. We were just splashing around on shore. My father was bald and he only had one hat, so when the wind picked his hat right off his head, and dropped it maybe twenty-five feet from shore, we didn't know what to do. Oscar volunteered to go, Gill was gonna go, George was gonna go, and I said I would go, but my father insisted, 'No, it is my hat; so I will be the one to go.' He appeared to just walk out there, pick up his hat, and walk back. Dad insisted that he could feel rocks under his feet where we knew there were no rocks before. Somehow his guardian angel delivered him safely to the hat, and then back to shore.'"

Granny Kiely had her hair done, and looked grand in her navy suit on the big day. She said she felt like the Queen Mum herself, and gave us a royal wave while she posed for a few pictures seated side-saddle on a Harley Davidson.

I was twenty-seven now, the mother of two, and all frilled up like a lilac southern belle. At a hundred and thirty-five pounds, I thought I was fat. In reflection I realize that was an illness. It's sad really. I had this weight goal in mind, but when I reached it, I still wasn't happy; never good enough. I didn't feel well on the morning of the wedding, especially when that nasty gas escaped from my behind as Gail was zipping up my dress. She pinched her nose, and said, "You're disgusting!"

I said, "I think I'm pregnant again."

The church windows and doors were wide open to welcome spring as we walked up to the altar. The lilac theme was a bust because what came early last year would arrive late this year. Father Christopher was giving his blessing when a blue swallow flew into the church, circled, and swooped over the crowd. During communion I followed a loud bumble bee, and smiled as Moira and Maureen were shooing and shushing it. Right in the middle of it all, I thought, "Birds, bees, I'm late. I've gotta be pregnant. I won't be doing any damage at the bar tonight. God, if I am pregnant, I hope this one is a boy, a healthy happy boy.'"

After the ceremony I followed the children out of Immaculate Conception Catholic Church in Sutton. When we caught up with Brad in his new suit waiting near the door, I said, "You bugger, I'm pregnant again."

Guests were amused by the fact that the Beer Store is conveniently located directly across the street. After a few cold ones, Brad swallowed the news, and appeared to be delighted with himself, going around calling himself, "Sure Shot."

During the speeches Dad commented on how good the bridesmaids looked with or without their clothes on. Then he tried to make good on his comment by insisting he meant we looked extra special today, but we look good in our jeans too.

Our first house - 1985

Jeannette and Rick dressed up Marie, and their new twin boys, Derek and Wayne, for the service. When I said our little white house was "The Cat's Ass", my Granny corrected me, saying it was "The Bee's Knees". She mentioned that I'd want to take better precautions to protect myself from having too many children.

Chapter Fourteen

Dylan as in Bob

My Da's knuckles rapped on the back door. When Brad opened it, he asked, "Can Pauline come out and play?" Dad had asked for my help earlier. He wanted me to go with him to The Upper Canada Mall to find a special gift for his wife. They would be celebrating twenty-five years of marriage tomorrow. He was wearing his *skull basher,* a tweed cap, and a mischievous grin because he was delighted with himself sporting her Visa. I was happy to get out of the house. It was a week night, and Brad could look after Lacey and LeeAnn for a few hours.

When our family had moved into the house on Highway 48, in 1974, Davis Drive was still a dirt road. I remember the spring the mud sucked the hub-caps off of my Father's convertible. In 1985 this main road leading to the town of Newmarket was paved, and the town of Newmarket had doubled in size since they had built The Mall. Dad said it was time for a diamond since my Mother had never had an engagement ring. We poked around in Sears and Mappins Jewellers but it was in People's where he got serious about purchasing an anniversary band. The rings we were shown were mostly a row of smaller diamonds meant to fit over or under a wedding ring. This was a great job for me because I got to try on the sparklers. He glanced over at the engagement ring display and said, "With my eyesight I can't see what all the fuss is about. Give us a look at that one there."

The woman working said, "Oh sir, that's a nice choice."

It was a wide band of yellow gold with three healthy stones across it, and he said, "I like this one. What do you think, Paul?" So I tried it on, smiled big, but said nothing because I didn't want to jinx it. He found it so funny that he had purchased her gift using her 'plastic', and couldn't understand why more and more stores these days weren't accepting cheques anymore. The ring was stunning, but I secretly wished that it had four stones. I knew my mother would be thrilled. Dad was really sentimental about their celebrating twenty-five years. He looked so proud walking through The Mall toting a big bag from People's with a tiny ring box inside.

My Mother said that he woke her up the next morning, because he couldn't wait to give her his gift. She wasn't comfortable wearing all these diamonds after all these years, and she kept referring to herself as 'Diamond Lil.' I was teasing them over coffee saying, "So since I was made in a car, and Mom mostly spoke French, and you with your Irish brogue I'm sure the attraction wasn't the conversation."

He said, "I'm not dead. What do you take me for? I'm a man, she's a woman, and that's what people do. Your mother and I were cut from the same cloth, just on different sides of the ocean; and we did talk too, Smarty-pants. We were consenting adults that both knew we were going to get married."

What they didn't know is that I had asked Father Christopher to come to the hall the night of their 25th Wedding Anniversary party to renew their vows. I was twenty-four, Colleen twenty, Sean eighteen, and Jim fourteen. I'd had a practice run as an event planner for my own wedding; so I booked the hall, mailed out the invitations, got permits, made lists, booked a D.J., and planned and prepared the food. Brad pretty much financially backed the entire venue, and the four of us held meetings to delegate jobs. We made back most of the expenses on the bar, but we didn't turn a profit or anything. My parents' dear friends, John and Susan Wright, were a big help. Susie, always very thoughtful, got great deals on decorations. *Big John Wright,* born in Yorkshire, England was my Dad's best friend.

The night of the big bash Mom and Dad went out for dinner with The Wrights; but since I had mailed our parents an invitation, they didn't have to act surprised. Some of the faces of old friends and neighbours surprised them though. My Mother wore a strapless, satin navy blue mermaid-style dress. It had a frill that ran down one side and trimmed the skirt. Dad was in a blue suit with a striped tie; and when his jacket came off, the tail of his shirt came out of the back of his trousers. He said he gave up on tucking it in years ago when he accepted the fact that he was long in the body. Her hair was short, brown, rolled, and sprayed to perfection. His hair was coarse, grey, and receding. She may have gained ten pounds tops in all these years, where as he was up at least fifty. He danced a chicken dance. They jived to *Rock Around the Clock* and enjoyed a cuddle when Elvis sang *Love me Tender.*

A standard buffet of cold meats, cheese, buns, pickles, crackers, veggies, coffee, cake and desserts was served during speeches. We chose Al James to be the emcee. He introduced long-time friends, Jerry Clancy, and John Wright, a plumber by trade, who said, "If you know nothing else, you know this; shit flows down hill, and pay day is Friday."

Auntie Anne who had been Mom's maid-of-honour said her bit, "Yolande and I shared an apartment. One day my Sister says to me, 'Wait until you meet my big man.' and this skinny kid is coming down the steps at the beach. She points at Kiely and says, 'There he is.' I started laughing, 'You call that a big man.' And then Yolande says, 'Well, he has big hands!'"

Al James closed with, "If you know John Kiely, you know he likes a good time, a good party. But what you don't know is that a couple of winters ago my pipes froze and burst, and our basement was flooding. It was three o'clock in the morning, on a miserable night, but the water was pouring in, and it was such a mess. I didn't know what to do; so I called my friend, John Kiely. This man got out of his warm bed, jumped in his truck, and drove forty minutes, to turn off our water and set up his sump-pump that cleaned up the mess. This is the kind of man that I today am very proud to call my friend. A toast to John and Yolande; congratulations, and here's to twenty-five more." I toasted with a ginger-ale because the four of us agreed no booze for us during the party.

The following spring Mom and Dad toured Europe for six weeks. That was their gift to each other. They returned with pictures from Spain and Switzerland, Rome and Italy. They'd had lunch in Paris, and played tourist in a place named Beaulieu in France. Mom especially loved France, while my Father appears delighted posing with monkeys in snap-shots at the Rock of Gibraltar.

When they returned they showed us plenty of photographs, and talked of vineyards, art galleries, churches, landmarks, and museums. At the end of this holiday they took a boat from France to Ireland. Dad said he couldn't be in Europe and not pop in and see his family. Mom said, "When we were on the boat, your Father didn't feel well. He was a bit hung-over, and sea-sick, and on his best behaviour because he was going to see his Mammy. I was partying with some of the Irish crew on the ship that were off duty. They were great fun: singing songs, telling jokes, and just yakking. Your Dad is there in his Aran sweater, and cap, but all sober and serious. So the girls kept saying, 'He can't be the Irish one. He's no fun. You're more Irish than him.' Then I said, 'He is the Irish one; I'm French Canadian!' And the one said, 'But you understand us. You know the lingo!' So I told her that's because I've been married to an Irishman for twenty-five years. I am Canadian, only Irish by injection. Then your Father said, 'It's time to call it a night, Lovey.'"

I thought I had arrived. I had cleaned up my act during my pregnancies, eating healthy and never drinking or smoking anything. When the girls were little I was only sneaking the odd drag around that time of the month, and drinking on social occasions. I had been blessed with healthy children and took this responsibility very seriously. I kept our house and children immaculate, and there was always a decent meal on the table.

LeeAnn's first word was "Button." She said it on a Sunday afternoon while her Grandpa was holding her perched on the fence. His horse, Rob Roy, came up and nipped a brown button off her Aran sweater and ate it. Her eyes were wide, and she just kept repeating, "Button! Button! Button!"

She and Lacey never said no about going to *The Farm*. They had a fifty-four inch television, and the girls would be entertained watching a VHS tape of the old classic musical, *Calamity Jane,* starring Doris Day and Howard Keel. The girls sang the songs, *Whip Crack Away* and *The Black Hills of Dakota*. Lacey was Calamity and LeeAnn the saloon girl, Katie Brown, for Halloween. Brad and I went to a fancy dress dance. I was a pretty pregnant witch, and he was super-cock. My husband wore yellow rubber gloves on his feet, long johns, a black t-shirt, red *Adidas* shorts and cape, and a rooster head mask.

If we walked to *The Farm* LeeAnn would break away from the pack in the last stretch, running ahead so she'd be first through the door to announce, "I'm here!" Sometimes she would wear her lace tights and rubber boots, and I would ask, "Where do you think you're going, Hollywood?"

Brad Parsons said he was a man on a mission, but his mission was different than that of paraplegic Rick Hanson's. Brad had been hurt very badly by the loss of his father. His emotions were all bottled up. Communication between us was poor and there was no whimsical light conversation. Brad was black and white - me and mine. He had been quite shy when I first met him, but grew louder with much more confidence as the years ticked by. Any humour that did come out of his mouth came in the form of sarcasm, usually at the expense of someone else. My Father said, "Sarcasm is the lowest form of wit."

I can't explain why I fell so hard for Brad except I was so naive and trying to make good for *my secret*. He was good-looking, and intelligent. He knew physics, and could figure out things like how much gas a car was burning as we drove down the road. Brad had more discipline than me, and was apprenticing to be a tool-and-die maker. I thought this was someone who painted tools. His brains, my personality - we would make awesome children, and we did. Images of my Father's red clamps or blue handles of axes came to mind when I heard tool-and-die maker. My Father said, "There are givers and takers in the world, and kid, you're a giver."

Lacey and LeeAnn - 1988

Brad wasn't home much at all during the third pregnancy. After watching a Disney movie with the girls called Toby Mc Teague, he said, "I'm going to look into that!" The flick was about sled dog racing. Brad wasn't very steady on a horse. I was the one who suggested he get a dog. He chose Arctic, a black male Siberian husky with ice-blue eyes. At nine months pregnant I endured the Minden Sled Dog Derby.

Brad had beat out all the other applicants for a higher-paying prestigious job. He was working twelve-hour shifts. Our kennel grew to three huskies, and then he had his social life. His sister was visiting once when he did call home from a strip club, "Honey, you should see the tight jeans in this place." Obviously he was drunk, but at least this time he remembered to call. I could hear the music pounding and murmur of voices in the background; and I smiled towards Brenda seated at our kitchen table.

"Pardon me? Brad, where are you? I asked.

"Out by the airport, and I don't think I'm gonna make it home. I've been invited to this after party out in Milton . . ." he slurred. "I'll be a good boy."

I trembled, and hot tears streamed down my cheeks as I hung up the phone. Brad would never know how much he hurt me because he really didn't care. He was twenty-nine years old, and he'd seen a lot of the real world while he was growing up: a dead man who hung himself in a tree, people pulling knives, men beating on women. As much as he said he loved me, a family on *The Farm* was like another world to him—a visit to Fantasy Island. When I did try to talk to him, he would glaze over and say, "The plane, Boss, the plane!"

I shared the conversation with his sister, collected myself, and we called it a night. I wondered, "If the shoe were on the other foot, would I want to live so close to his family?"

My mother said, "Women tend to think with their hearts, and men tend to think with their dicks." I found this so coarse. She also said, "If I could put a forty-year-old brain on a twenty-year-old body, I'd have it made." This I thought to be wise.

My Mother overheard Lacey tell LeeAnn that Grandpa was a giant, like Gulliver. Besides the two girls and the baby on the way, I had plenty to consume my time and energy. I was driving a small school bus for grocery money. My route included out-of-the-way places and some special-needs children. There were fifteen passengers in all, and two were my own children. LeeAnn was still in her car seat, and she often dozed off. When the bus was empty on sunny days, the three of us would sing at the tops of our lungs. It was a perfect job for me, especially given the fact it followed the school year.

Marsha and Otto had moved into Newmarket. I had grown very close to her and missed her radiant energy very much. Mini and I made gingerbread houses at Christmas time, and she inspired and taught me to paint folk art; after some lessons I showed others how to paint. By following the simple steps we produced some really impressive pieces. Dad commissioned me to paint a dozen *Welcome Ducks* for his customers that year. He said they'd be more effective if they had *Welcome* on one side and *Get Lost* on the other.

The new neighbours were Phil, Heather, and little Amanda Sauer. The Sauer's daughter was adorable; but their dog, not so adorable. Bennie managed to climb Brad's kennel fence, and lock onto one of his two new female huskies, the sisters, Shannon and Sabrina. The night my water broke and I went into labour, Shannon had delivered one big pup that afternoon. Brad wasn't in any hurry to get to the hospital. He shot some video of the scene before taking his shower.

Dylan Charles Parsons was born without complications in the early hours of January 12, 1988. The baby was gorgeous, weighing eight pounds four ounces. I saw my hairline, and my Father's nose and lips. I remembered that I had mentioned to the Creator that it would be good if this one was more like me because I didn't suffer with allergies. I'd had faith he would be my boy since my request at the altar.

I chose this name because there weren't many I'd come to admire in the world, but the poetry and lyrics of singer-songwriter Bob Dylan stirred something deep inside me. My Dylan would eat, sleep, poop, smile, eat, clap hands, poop, smile, eat, sleep, jolly jump, smile, poop, sleep. Honestly, it's all a blur. I asked Lacey if she remembers her Father being around the house much. Did she remember him ever giving her a bath? She said, "Yes, once, when Dylan was a baby." The girls were four and three at the time and their hair was to their waists. "He took a towel, and he rubbed it back and forth over our heads.

When we had our pyjamas on and came to say goodnight to you and Dylan, you got upset because our hair was all tats."

Christmases were always made special. Dylan's first word was "Birdie," so he got a canary from Santa that year. No one but Brad and I really knew how 'functioning dysfunctional' our relationship was. I'd had a phone call from a sly woman, who said, "Mrs. Parsons, I work with Brad, and I think you should know he is having an affair."

I said, "Well, the lucky girl, he's great in the sack."

"Mrs. Parsons, I'm not joking, Brad is having an affair . . . with Cheri."

"Honey, I know Cheri. You don't know me. If Brad is having an affair, it must be with you because Cheri, as nice as she is, isn't Brad's type."

The caller hung up. So I dialled his work number, and was connected to Brenda at reception. "I'd like to speak to Cheri, please. Hi, Cheri. Brad's wife, Pauline. I just had a call from some twit in your office who says you're having an affair with Brad."

"I know who it was. That bitch! Pauline, I am not the one having an affair.

"I knew it wasn't you. You're too smart to get involved with a married man."

Upon arriving home, Brad told me my call to Cheri had stirred up quite a scene. After she hung up, Cheri had walked right up to this temp and slapped her hard across the face.

Sadie Darcy had met John Pilgrim, and she had the bling. They had set the date, and I would be bridesmaid for the last time. We were on the wedding circuit. Between the Beaulieu side, friends our age, and the big splash for a "Kiely Wedding" it was like a second career. Thomas Darcy had made Colleen a five-tier wedding cake. How many tiers for his kid sister, Sadie, who was now working for him at his Bradford Italian Bakery.

LeeAnn was an independent and comical child. One summer evening she painted herself red in lipstick, then came bouncing out the back door in her panties and pearls and shouted, "Surprise!" When I went into the house there were her smudged little footprints on the stairs and toilet seats. I guessed she was checking in the mirrors to make sure she was still red before yelling "Surprise!" The mess was fresh and easy to clean with Lestoil. When our little star was four, in junior kindergarten, she says to me, "Mom, I think you better get a couple of pizzas and a cake for Friday night."

LeeAnn - 1988

I asked, "Why?"

"Because it's my birthday, and I'm having a party. Lacey and I made the invitations and gave them out on Monday."

It was a good thing I got the pizza and cake, balloons, and some loot bags because her little friends all showed up. It was a Friday night so when Brad came home with a two-four of beer, we got to know Jessie's parents better. Cathy worked for a bank, and Roger was also a tool-and-die maker; and after the kids party, in no time at all the four of us had all drunk our share of that beer. Jessie, Roger, and Cathy slept in the spare room and left early the following morning.

On St. Patrick's Day I invited my parents over for dinner. I served T-bone steaks, baked potatoes, and broccoli with cheese, carrots, and apple pie with ice cream. After we stuffed ourselves, my Father said, "That was very good, but it wasn't Irish. Maybe you and Brad need to visit your Granny? She'll teach you to cook a corned beef and cabbage. Why don't you go up to Sutton Travel and look into the charter fares for early May, my treat. If you want to take Dylan he flies free. It's up to you, but a baby will slow you down; and trust me, if you're wanting to show my Mother the baby, she has seen her share. What do you think, Lovey? You and I could look after the twerps for a couple of weeks!"

So I stopped eating big meals and sweets, and walked around the block a country mile to knock off the baby weight. In late May I was tanned and trim when Brad and I rode the moving sidewalk at Heathrow Airport. Moira and Rory greeted us with tight squeezes and kisses. They drove us to their home in Suffolk. I was nodding off at the table from the jet lag so Brad and I took a nap. When I woke up Moira had drawn me a bath, and made me a cup of sweet tea. We had a chat with their lot, and we walked around enjoying ice-creams at the scenic Tudor village of Lavenham. I marvelled when Rory stopped his car on the side of the road. Moira got out, walked through the gate of a white picket fence, and plucked lettuce and tomatoes fresh from someone's garden. My aunt put some silver coins in a tin, got back into the car, and we drove off with the fresh produce.

Brad and I took a train from Euston station in London through Wales to Hollyhead. The plush upholstered reclining train seats were much more comfortable than they had been twenty years before. The sleek train had large windows and a sunroof to take in the Welsh countryside. I had turned green on the Sea Link ferry, and felt that I was going to lose my breakfast until I spotted the spires of Dun Laoghaire. I was wearing my Aran sweater; and when we came into port I was the first person down the ramp. Maureen and Harry were in Ireland on holiday; and they were there, with Aunts Kate and Maggie, Tina, Jenny, Colm, and Ellen. I felt so special that they had all come to meet us. I was surrounded, but what was whacking my ankles? I looked down and saw the end of a cane that led to herself. "Granny! Even Granny came to meet me." I said, and my heart was so full.

Brad and I spent a few days in Bray with Maggie, Charlie, and the kids, then a few days in Killiney with Auntie Kate, and her black Lab, Onyx. But it was in Dalkey where I had the best steak of my life. Pan fried in butter, and prepared to perfection by my Grandmother who lovingly served the meat with boiled spuds and mushy peas. When Brad and I stayed at her house we changed a few burnt-out light bulbs, and I slipped in some new tea towels. I had to laugh at the way Granny let the peelings from the spuds hit the floor, and then took the broom and swept them out the back door into the garden for the birds.

At the table Granny gulped two glasses of wine, and says she, "The Grandfather was a character indeed. After his dear missus passed he'd often come round here for his Sunday tea. Jack would be away, and his old fella would say to me, 'Lizzy, an ole steak will do me anyday.' And me with a full house of mouths to feed, and a pot of stew on the boil. I'd be t'inking, 'An ole steak, me arse.'"

The following morning as Granny was getting washed, she said, "I wash up to possible, down to possible, and then possible." Later as we were strolling along she said, "You can shop and shop, but all that glitters is not gold; or you can pray and pray, but at times I do wonder if He is hard of hearing." We ducked into a chapel for a rest, and says she to me, "For the life of me, I don't understand why the church is always asking for money. The statues don't eat a thing, nor do they require any heat. We take nothing with us when we go, child, and we become only memories in the hearts we've touched along the journey."

On the flight home I sat next to a young American woman that was travelling with three little girls. After we knocked back a few Baileys on ice, she whispered to me that she was a gunrunner for the IRA. We started singing rebel songs:

A hungry feeling, came over me stealing,
and the mice they were squealing, all in my cell.
And the auld triangle went jingle jangle
all along the banks of the Royal Canal.

In the early morning, the screws were bawlin'
saying get up you bowsie's and clean out yer cells!
And the auld triangle went jingle jangle
all along the banks of the Royal Canal.

Well the line was sleeping, and Begussy was peepin'
as I lay there dreamin' of my girl Sal.
And the auld triangle went jingle jangle
all along the banks of the Royal Canal.

In the female prison, there are seventy-five women,
and I wished among them that I did dwell.
And the auld triangle could go jingle jangle
all along the banks of the Royal Canal.

Brad said, "You might want to tone it down. For Christ's sake, the holiday is over."

I was feeling no pain, and said, "It is not, not till we get off this plane. Then I, with my loud Irish whisper, said, "Want to join the mile high club?"

"Are you serious?"

I said, "Sure, you only live once. Go into the washroom and I'll knock twice, and you can let me in."

I was wearing a denim dress that fastened up the front with domes. We bumped and ground in the tiny space, and then I got tidied up, but was still flushed and blushed when I opened the door and slammed it closed again. There was a line-up waiting to use the washroom. Brad turned the lock back to occupied, and he gave me time to return to my seat. He was in a much better mood when he returned to his seat. My drinking buddy had passed out.

This trip was my Father's way of saying thank you for their twenty-fifth anniversary party, and for looking after things while they'd been touring Europe. It was a shot in the arm. Although it ended on a positive note, once we were back home our frigid relations resumed. Brad went fishing alright, but for blondes. He never brought home one fish or even a fishing tale.

In June 1990 I would be twenty-nine, and my sister was ready to pop with her first child. It was a long day and a great effort on her part, but she came through with an eight-pound-six-ounce baby boy, Ryan Richard Duffy. At the hospital Colleen had insisted all day that she was having this kid on her sister's birthday, and the nurses had said to her, "Your sister must be very important."

"I just looked at them like they should know this. You are important, Paul, important to me."

Their bambino was a bam-bam that was stuck, but Colleen watched the clock, huffed and puffed, and came through. Ryan's bassinet card read "Duffy Ryan Richard born June 12th, 1990, at 11:59 p.m." My Mother was the first to be introduced to him, and she christened him "Tuxon," a French slang word meaning 'a robust little man'.

When I did turn the dreaded thirty the following year, Brad threw a huge party for me. We had the luxury of a fire-pit in the pasture behind our house. We were famous for our parties. We'd have Colleen and Cam's friends, Sean's and Jim's friends, plus the cousins, and our own friends. A lot of people must have been there because we got over sixty bucks return in empties. There was a live band set up on the hay wagon. I was drunk most of the day before the party, and still in a fog on my real birthday. Not pretty.

Brad had some friends from work there. This hose-bag Mia was all over him. She wore a pendant of a kitty with emerald eyes around her neck, a neck I would have liked to strangle. He threw another girl friend from his work in our above ground pool. In doing so he bent his knee back and was hurt pretty bad. People thought he should have it checked, go to the hospital, but honestly I didn't care.

While we were out riding one afternoon my Father planted the seed of building a new house on the wet lot. He had no idea how bad things were between Brad and me, but had said out loud that he felt like the children's surrogate father, and my surrogate husband. My Mom and Calamity Jane babysat the children a lot when he and I were riding. 'The Lord and Master' had two lots for sale on *The Farm* in 1991, two acres on Prout road, and four acres of wetland on the other side of the tracks. Dad didn't have nearly as much invested into this wet lot because the train track was a natural severance. He had to pay twenty grand in survey fees for the two acres that was listed for eighty-grand. The view wasn't quite as scenic in the valley, but he said that he couldn't just give it to me, that he wanted something for the four acres. He figured twenty-five grand was more than fair.

While I was thinking about all of this and working on Brad about the prospect of building a new house, I had a dream that Uncle George came to see me. The next day my Dad popped by early in the morning and he said, "I didn't sleep well last night, and you can have that lot or the other one if you want it."

I asked, "What's gotten into you? Did you have a visit from Uncle George or something?"

He said, "How did you know?"

So I told him about my dream.

I wanted this new house. It gave me something else to focus on. I knew there was an economic recession happening as my brothers and brother-in-law were out of work. This was a win-win because they needed jobs, and we were up to about twenty-seven huskies now. The howling when Brad fed wasn't appreciated by anyone, especially by the folks next door who had a new baby. Generally, Brad would feed late at night because of his schedule. For us a new house on this wet lot made perfect sense. There was a vein of gravel on *The Farm* for fill, and with the train whistle blowing hourly, nobody could complain about our dogs.

With an ad in the Toronto market, savvy real estate agent, Penny Politeski, managed to sell our house for that magic sum of a hundred and fifty thousand dollars. She used a catch phrase that read, "As rare as hen's teeth." We would all have to live at *The Farm* while the new house was under construction. Brad went to work moving his kennel as soon as the offer was firm. The single woman who bought our home got our best mouser too. My tabby cat refused to leave the *Bee's Knees*.

The Politeski's were a lively bunch. They lived in a century fieldstone house on the Prout Road. My Mother, frustrated with farm-living, had gone out for a cross-country ski when she first met Mrs. Politeski, or "The Princess" as her hubby Don called her. He was a pilot with Air Canada, mostly national cargo flights. She was an Aussie, and they had married later in life after a whirlwind romance touring Europe in an MG which now rested under a tarp in their barn. They'd had four children in five years: Justin, Andrew, Christine, and Matt, all between Sean and Jim's age.

While sipping a glass of wine or two, Penny showed my mother around their farmhouse and she exclaimed, "I'm madly in love with the place."

My Mother said, "Well, woman, either you're crazy or I am, but if you can't beat them, join them!" And she returned home repeating, "I'm madly in love with this place!" But we knew it was the wine because she wasn't madly in love with the place. Mom did love her central vac. She would suck up dead flies by the hundreds. There was a garter snake she called Slippery Sid that made eerie appearances in the stone wall of the basement, mice, and one big old bat in the attic for excitement. *The Farm* was not my mother's cup of tea. She preferred coffee. When my Dad tried to coax her to come out to the barn, she put that little French foot down, "If I go into that barn, the next thing I know I'm milking cows. This is your pipe dream, John Kiely, not mine. If anyone would had told me I'd be living on a farm, I'd have said, never."

Mom did have a smile on her face driving the tractor when we were doing hay. She slugged like the rest of us in the mow, singing;

> *"Green Acres is the place to be.*
> *Farm living is the life for me,*
> *Land spreading out so far and wide.*
> *Keep Manhattan, just give me that countryside."*

She was almost proud of herself when she ran over Dad's foot. The ground was soft so he wasn't hurt. The grandkids enjoyed riding on the tractors and hay wagons. We all did.

Our home was kept clean, and freshly decorated. Our children were fed healthy meals and snacks, and they had plenty of fresh air and exercise. I didn't get drunk that often, but when I did, I sure did. Brad housed his dogs in old whiskey barrels. If they were fresh ones he'd add some water, swish it around and make barrel wash before cutting the end off and placing the barrel on a stand for a dog's house. He said it wasn't as strong as the real stuff. One Saturday night after the kids and the guys were sleeping, Colleen and I got into the swish.

We drank what we called 'the Holy Water' and talked for hours and hours. It was dawn, getting light outside, and we had a brilliant idea! We were going to walk to *The Farm* and go riding. We shushed each other as we fumbled out the back door.

The dew was heavy, the air fresh and crisp, but we couldn't feel a thing. I told my sister I loved her, and she said I was the best. We walked the "Winnie the Pooh" trail through the cedars and then through a hayfield before reaching the corn field. It was the end of August and the corn was tall and full of spiders. The new guy planting the fields had failed to leave us our trails this year. I put my arms up, picked a lane, and I ran into the corn and burst out the other side. I sat on a fence rail and waited for my sister. I waited and waited; then I finally shouted, "Colleen, are you alright?"

"Is there an end to this?" she yelled back.

I said, "Pull up a stock and hold it up so I can see where you are."

A corn stalk popped up about thirty feet away. I said, "I can see you. Keep holding it up, and follow the sound of my voice." She did, and appeared dazed and confused when she emerged. The horses were annoyed that we woke them up, and put their bridles on. Drunk or sober, my sister and I would always sing to our horses:

"I ride an old paint. I lead an old dan.
I'm going to Montana to throw a hooligan.
They feed in the coolie, they water in the draw.
Their tails are all matted, and their backs are all raw.
Ride around, ride around real slow,
for the firey and the scruffy are rarin' to go.
Well when I die, take my saddle from the wall.
Put it on my pony and lead her from the stall.
Tie my bones to her back, and turn our faces to the west,
and we'll ride the prairie that we love the best!
Ride around . . . ride around real slow,
for the firey and the scruffy are rarin' to go!"

Pauline Kiely on her sister's horse Bailey - 1992

I loved Linda Ronstadt's version of this song, and for an encore we faithfully sang Willie Nelson's, *Red-Headed Stranger*. There are four verses, but it's the last one that's the clincher;

> *"She followed him out as he saddled the stallion and laughed as she grabbed at the bay.*
> *He shot her so quick there was no time to warn her, she never heard anyone say;*
> *Don't cross him, don't boss him, he's wild in his sorrow,*
> *He's riding, hiding his pain.*
> *Don't fight him, don't spite him, just wait till tomorrow, maybe he'll ride on again.*

The yellow-haired lady was buried at sunset.
The stranger went free of course,
Cause you can't hang a man for killing a woman who was
  trying to steal his horse!
This is the tail of the Red-Headed Stranger,
and if he should pass your way,
Stay outta the path of that raging black stallion, and don't
  lay a hand on the bay.

We fancied ourselves cowboys, but really we were more like Indians, wearing suede moccasins, fringed coats, and riding bareback.

Dad chauffeured when we rode together to a bridal shower three hours away in Woodstock. He would talk farmer with Bruce while Aunt Anne served cabbage rolls, and her daughter opened her gifts. Lacey, LeeAnn, Colleen, Mom, and I all were seated comfortably in the navy blue Caprice Classic that was my Mother's grocery-getter. Mom had wiped out the Caddy by slamming on the breaks to avoid hitting a little dog; and cursed herself afterwards for not killing that stupid little dog because she nearly killed herself. She had given Jim her Chevette because she was tired of driving kids.

The drive home on the 401 east was dark, and raining. On a Sunday night the traffic was heavy. In the dark, in the center of highway traffic, a guy was sitting on the hood of his car waving a white T-shirt around his head. My Dad pulled over on the side of the highway, and we could feel the tires grab when he hit the brakes. Wind from the passing cars and trucks made our car rock like a boat.

"Did you see that?" he said as he backed up on the shoulder of the 401 in the dark.

I said, "I'm not comfortable with this, Dad."

"Someone needs help back there!"

My Father put the car in park, opened his door, and squeezed out. Then we watched him dodge the cars that misted him with rain as they whizzed by at ninety miles an hour. When he got back into the car, he said, "That poor bugger's been out there for hours."

While Dad was cleaning his glasses, the back door opened. The interior lights came on, and we scrunched over so this guy could fit into our car. This guy was a big tattoo'd black man who kept saying, "Thanks, man. Thanks, man. No really, thanks, man."

Dad offered him twenty bucks when he got out at the nearest gas station, but he said, "No thanks, man. Just thanks, man. Me and the Missus have been out there since two o'clock this afternoon, and she's got the baby in the car." Our ride home was quiet after that, and I was very proud of my Father.

Chapter Fifteen

The Dog Named Dalkey

T he day her brother announced he had chosen to stop drinking alcohol, Auntie Theresa said, "This is a sad day indeed!" Dad said he couldn't stand the hangovers anymore. He had just turned fifty, and told his doctor that his guts were in bits. The doctor told him that his body was producing too much iron. His guts were never the same after the tractor accident, and I noticed how he had aged. His thinking was old school. He refused to speak to answering machines, and had no time or tolerance for computers.

Dad said, "I guess I've had my share of the liquid gold. I'm done."

We kept his birthday to the immediate family. Now that Dad was on his best behaviour, it was awkward being around his drinking buddies. Colleen and Cameron showed up with a big present all wrapped up with ribbons and bows. This box was the size of a television, and Cameron recommended this gift be opened outdoors. When Dad touched it, the box moved. He said, "What the hell, is there something alive in here?" As he tore into the box, four laying hens flew out.

We had all pitched in a bit of money and bought our Father a gold Claddagh ring. He sure brought us back our share of them. I'd had a silver one with a Connemara marble stone in the center. My brothers and Colleen wore silver Claddagh's, and Mom had a flashy one with small diamonds surrounding an emerald in the heart. We figured even if the Irishman wasn't one for jewellery, he may wear a Claddagh – stamped 'Made in Ireland'.

The symbol of the Claddagh is over three hundred years old, and has become very popular. It appears as a heart with a crown on it being held in a set of hands. Dad said it was an old Irish wedding ring that meant, "In my hands I hold your heart and crown it with my love." Other references say that this Claddagh symbol means love, friendship, and loyalty.

John Kiely - 1991

My Da was a boob man, and he mentioned more than once that he had this fantasy about walking through a field of 'diddies' in his bare feet. For his fiftieth birthday I got pink balloons and blew them up just right, and then I taped them in pairs so the illusion was there. When he arrived I blind-folded him and told him to take his socks off. Then I led him into the room and removed the blind fold. Delighted, he stomped on the balloons, laughing his ass off. After a meal, we went to The Red Barn Theatre and caught a Yuk Yuks Comedy Show.

Maureen nicknamed my old man 'the Squire' because John F. Kiely was the second name on the deed and title of *The Farm*. With the four of us pretty much raised for better or worse, Dad said he bought the cottage to practice for retirement. I think it was a retreat, a quiet place to hide once in a while. It was a three-bedroom brick bungalow on Moore Lake in Haliburton.

John Kiely on the porch of the new house - 1992

On St. Patrick's Day in 1992 we wanted to get my Father something special for building us our dream house. I decided on a very special gift, just what he had always wanted, an Irish Setter puppy. At Queensville Farm Supply my Da had met a dark golden retriever. This gorgeous animal was all he talked about. "That was some beauty dog. Jainey, what a lovely dog! The only t'ing that would've made that dog better was if he was red." My Father's Big Red was registered as 'the Squire's Dalkey'.

Brad, I, and our kids drove four hours to a kennel to get him this Irish Setter puppy. I picked the biggest of the two litters on display in children's playpens. Dad used to say, "I may have been a Texan in another life. I like things big like J.R." Brad had brought one of his dog crates in the back of our clubcab pick-up truck, but the Paddy who sold us the pup took one look at the situation and commented, "This isn't a feckin' sled dog. You can't put this guy in a crate, in the back of your truck out in the cold. He's meant to be your mate, your companion, and he certainly isn't in tune with this climate."

When we arrived at *The Farm,* Dad came out looking pissed off. The kids ran ahead, and he said, "Where the hell have you lot been? Here it is Paddy's Day."

"We brought you a present, Grandpa." Lacey said, "It's an Irish Setter puppy."

"Really."

When I got out of the truck and handed Da his six-week old Squire's Dalkey, he said, "That's not an Irish Setter." And he immediately passed the dog to my Mother.

Mom said, "Thanks, thanks a lot. Really, for me!" and she pretended her index finger was a pistol, and she said, "bang, bang." as she pretended to shoot herself in the temple.

We loved the handsome pup. He had personality plus and soon took his place in the family. At first Super Tramp, too old now to play, wasn't sure about the new kid; but even he couldn't resist Dalkey's charm. Dad boiled his "boy-yo" an egg in the mornings and served it with toast. Dalkey did all those wonderful puppy things: tinkles in the hall, chewing Mom's shoes, and barn cat chasing. He was a food processor that grew big fast. Dalkey would pluck apples and pears off the fruit trees and eat them.

The excitement happened when Big Red was about a year old, in mid January of 1993. We had made arrangements to stay at the cottage situated nearer the bottom of Moore Lake at the mouth of Gull River. Brenna, Dan, and Alicia had joined us at the Coboconk Frost Festival. We had a day at the winter carnival where Brad and Alicia were racing dog teams.

Saturday night around 10:30 p.m., Dalkey was put out in the garage. We thought the door was down, and closed. Ten minutes later we realized the door was up, and Dalkey was gone.

Dad immediately ran down to the lake because he knew how his dog loved the water. The shore line was frozen for about a hundred feet out, and then the water was open because of the current. We couldn't see anything until we got a light. Out there in the black we saw his glowing eyes, his head above the ice. He was breathing heavily, and there was mist coming out of his mouth as he whined and cried for help. How long had he been out there? How long could he hang on? How could we save him?

We ran around in circles crying and upset, "Hang on, Dalkey!" We looked for boats, but they were frozen or away for the winter. My husband, Uncle, Aunt, Mom, I, and especially Dad felt sick and so upset. This was awful, but what could we do? The ice was dangerously thin. Dad ran frantically into the cottage and came out shouting, "Hang on, buddy! Hang on, Dalkey!" He had taken a door off its hinges, and grabbed a boat paddle. He cut the rope from the flag pole, tied it around his waist and said, "Hang on to me, boys."

Brad said, "John, don't go out there."

Then he and Dan picked up the rope, and said, "All for one."

Sliding along on the door, Dad got to be inches away from his dog, but Dalkey, with his back end frozen, couldn't help himself. Then the ice broke away . . . and the dog went down. We could hear the bubbles of air reach the surface from shore. My Dad had his head down, sobbing.

Uncle Dan said, "He's gone, John. Let him go. Back up now and come to shore."

My Mom, Brenna, and I just watched. I fell to my knees and said, "God, my Dad is a good man. Why are you taking his dog from him?" and had finished a full *Our Father* when suddenly Dalkey came up and bit on to the end of my Father's outstretched fingers. His natural reflex jerked his hand back, then he grabbed the leather collar and shouted, "I got him!"

We couldn't believe it when he stood up and dragged his frozen friend to shore. Dad's footprints in the snow on the ice were soon filled by water. Embracing Dalkey, he said, "I'm 52 years old. Are you trying to give me a heart attack?" He carried his dog into the cottage, and we wrapped him in blankets and rubbed his body for an hour until he could walk.

The Squire's Dalkey - 1994

The following morning I told the children about all the excitement the night before. They hugged their Granddad. It was a very emotional moment for them to see him with the band-aids on his fingers, and with his dog that wouldn't leave his side. They hugged their Grandpa who said, "It never ceases to amaze me what faith, hope, love, and a little Irish luck can do."

My new dream house became a lonely nightmare. With the exception of Annette, Liz, Ruthie, and Laurie coming on Tuesday nights to paint, I didn't have much going for me. Our North Force Sled Dog kennel, sponsored by a major pet food company, was up over sixty dogs now. Brad was generally gone training, or to a race, or to talk dog somewhere. On the outside I faked happy, but on the inside I felt as I did back when I was fifteen, isolated and depressed.

My husband's November birthday was just a dreadful night. It was pouring rain when Jane, a mutual friend, came knocking at our door. I had gone to school with her, and now she was a temp at Brad's factory. She had her three kids with her, and a tray of fresh warm cinnamon buns that she had baked from scratch for him because, as she said, "I heard you weren't into baking."

Brad was resting by the fireplace with LeeAnn. His hair was sticking up, and he didn't smell so good as he'd just returned and eaten after training dogs in the rain. For his birthday I'd cooked a roast beef dinner with Yorkshire pudding, and a homemade cherry cheese cake for dessert. I offered her a cup of tea and a generous piece of cake. This wasn't the first time she had come for a visit, but it was the first time she'd ventured out in the night, and a night like this. The kids knew each other and had retreated to the other room.

It was awkward. She couldn't stay long, and they left within the hour. It was still raining when I closed the door and bid them good night, and it was still raining when I went into the kitchen and began pitching buns at Brad, shouting, "You want Jane, and her God damn cinnamon buns. Why don't you just say it? Why won't you just say you want a divorce? Why do you insist on driving me crazy with your girl friends and fucking dogs! One horse, one saddle, that's all you need. Jesus Christ, sixty-eight dogs! Where's all the money going, Brad?"

Our family did have some great days at Copeland Forest racing huskies, but now Brad was into Alaskan Huskies that were a greyhound cross. His goals were high.

When he sold the fifty-five Chevy for a dog truck, I knew it was serious. Dan and Brenna lived near Copeland. They had six huskies that they raced for recreation. Alicia was delighted to have the company of the girls, and we were treated to 'Gildener hospitality' that included a hot-tub, hearty food, a few glasses of wine when we stayed there.

Brenna and Dan moved out that way, and their family worked long days at their gas station business for about seven years. When they sold the business they had a nice home built at Bluewater Beach. It was sandy beaches in the summer time, and very tranquil during winter months, buried in deep snow. Large individual flakes fell, and some of the roads had limited access because the drifts were so high.

We had met some really nice people dog racing: The Lang's, Le Duc's, and Hillcrest's. It had a family atmosphere and was a healthy day outside, well actually two days because results were based on a combination time. The Siberian Husky Club had kid and mutt races on Sundays after the four and eight dog classes. Dylan went to races as a baby in diapers. He only cried when his fingers got cold or his bum got wet. They'd all had a turn at winning kid and mutt. We called LeeAnn, Natasha, because she had this Russian-looking pink hat with faux white fur around it. Lacey was her dad's best helper. Dylan won a trophy with his old Siberian boy, Keys. We went to races all over the place; and I felt like maybe dog sledding was Brad's last ditch at trying to make our marriage work. I couldn't make any sense of the dogs. There were too many mouths to feed.

Dogs and money were being hustled. Numbers and demands were on the rise. This was a big load. I was so busy but felt empty, hollow. I had so much on my plate that I didn't have time to think or feel. When I read Albert Einstein's quote, "The definition of insanity is doing the same thing over and over, but expecting a different result", a light came on. Things between Brad and me certainly weren't getting any better, yet I was running day after day, year after year, like a hamster on a wheel.

I asked Brad, "What are your plans for the next three to five years? Where do you see yourself, that sort of thing?"

His reply was all about his dog lines and pedigrees, races he was planning to win. He continued to speak but I didn't continue to listen. I cut him off by saying, "You never mention me or the kids. You never can make it to their school concerts. You don't help me with dentist appointments or anything, really. Jesus Christ, Brad, it's all about you; and this is a fucking dog concentration camp. The kids have to open forty cans of food every night. We mix it with bone meal, fish oil, ground chicken, and supplements, and then we eat cans of soup. This is ridiculous! On a school bus driver's salary you expect me to feed and support three kids."

My nerves were shot. My weight bloomed, and when I hurt my shoulder, I had to stop bus driving. After physiotherapy, I took a job bartending at The Briar's Inn and Country Club in Jackson's Point. This five star resort was about my best option given the kids were still in school in Sutton at St. Bernadette's. The gorgeous setting and just being with other adults in the work force was a real treat.

One day my children love to remind me of is the day I completely forgot about them. As once again our cupboards were bare, I said I would bring them a nice lunch at school, drop it off on my way to work. I used to do this once in a while. It had worked out well after the morning bus run to pop over to the IGA and get them a treat, like a *Lunchable*, and a round of chocolate milks. I don't know how, but this once I completely forgot about lunches. When the three of them came home at four-thirty, they stomped into the house, and plunked themselves down in front of me.

"Thanks a lot." Lacey said. "We waited near the door by the office for our Mother who said she was bringing us a great lunch today, but she never showed up. The teachers gave us stuff from their lunches, and asked our classmates if they had anything to share. Nice one, Mom."

Forget lunch one day and they never forget it; make lunch for ten years and nobody remembers. I felt terrible. My mind was racing with so many thoughts. I was working shifts; Brad still worked twelve hour shifts and he was a glutton for overtime. Still there was never enough time or money.

I remembered how he used to go fishing, but we never ate fish. I knew a guy that went fishing with them, and he didn't come home with any fish either. He did come home with a case of crabs, though. Things were really crazy, and a lot of people were snorting cocaine in the eighties. I didn't get it, and when I found some of my so-called-friends doing lines, I was shocked. I asked, "Why hasn't anybody ever offered that shit to me?"

Someone who would wish to remain anonymous replied, "Because it makes you talk more, and dance more, and honestly you're already high voltage on booze."

I enjoyed my black hash. It just took the edge off and slowed things down, but I could still function. I preferred to smoke because I was actually socially retarded too many times, ridiculously drunk in public. I had this idea that I should be proud to be Irish; therefore, I should drink alcohol, be loud, dance, and sing songs until I fell down or blacked out.

"You showed her how to drink, and I showed her how to smoke," Mom said.

Dad said, "The only thing I would change in my life is the drinking. And to make it worse, today there are drugs. A junkie will kill for his drugs, while most drunks will just beg for a drink. I've given up the sauce, so when are you going to give up those dirty cigarettes?"

"When I'm good and ready," Mom replied.

"Yolande, it's like you taking a hammer and whacking your thumb. Your thumb is yellow, then green, black, and then blue, but you keep whacking it. What do those filthy things do for you? Stink up your breath, burn your money, and cause feckin' cancer."

"It's not that bad, Paul. Everybody else is drunk too." Colleen said.

I'd made a complete ass of myself at Brad's company Christmas party. I managed to score a second bottle of wine for our table by providing a close up of my cleavage to this twenty-year-old kid working the bar. We needed a new bottle because I'd pretty much drunk the first one.

Brad said, "Are you some kind of a moron? Really, are you stupid or something? You Catholics are all hypocrites. You get hammered on Saturday night and then go to church and pray for forgiveness every Sunday. Really, you disgust me. You've gotten so fat, and you wear your hair like an old lady."

The bevelled glass in the doors cast rainbows throughout the main floor when the sun shone through the Pella windows of my dream house. There were six bevelled glass doors. Sean and I had drawn the first drafts of the floor plan on a napkin. He was pretty proud of himself when his drawings got the stamp of approval from the Township.

Dad would say, "This isn't a recession. It's a depression."

He blamed the bad economy on Mulroney, and stressed over Free Trade. I knew nothing of politics. When our family was at Mass, the parish priest announced that he wouldn't baptise children unless their parents attended Mass for six weeks. We didn't know what was going on but suddenly Dad stood up and loudly said, "Father, where I come from God's love is unconditional, and babies are baptised as soon as possible. It is the child's right as it is a child of God, and without sin. It isn't because the parents attend Mass, nor for a priest to decide."

While building our house my Father was able to teach his sons their trade. Mom and I are the only ones who really remembered building Ballantrae and the house on Forty-eight. We made construction fun by serving theme lunches, and speaking with fake accents. While imitating a French-Canadian framing crew, Sean called himself Jacque La Roc, Jim was Gaston, and

Cameron, John Claude. They'd let the stubble grow on their chins and talked like, "You dere, you pass me dat hammer, eh." When they did the duct work they were German; and electrical, Dutch; while tiling they took on Italian accents, and called themselves Gino, Vito, and Luigi. We were Wops for a good three weeks, and because my family and I were living at *The Farm* with my parents and my brothers, it carried on after hours. Of course, when it came to the cabinets, hanging doors, and trimming out, they were Irish.

On St. Patrick's Day we watched a young Sean Connery in *Darby O'Gill and The Little People* on the big screen. Darby, attempting to stay ahead of the Banshee and the funeral coach, managed to scare the piss out of a second generation. My mother said, "Dylan's Indian name would be 'Two Cookies', because every time that kid comes in to the kitchen he says, "Memère, can I have two cookies?"

For the first time I tried French pea soup and I made the mistake of asking, "Mom, how come we've never had this stuff before?"

She gave me that look and my answer. "Pauline, do you know how much French pea soup I ate when I was a kid? My mother went through a fifty pound bag of peas every winter."

I saw the hurt in my Father's eyes when he asked Brad to give him a hand with something and he arrogantly replied, "I get paid for what I know, not what I do. I'm no ignorant grunt worker."

Chapter Sixteen

Horse Mad

The melting snow and song of the red-winged black bird gave me hope in the spring of 1993. As I often did, I caught myself thinking about the clan in Ireland. I wondered if they, too, were enjoying a fine spring day. I decided to call Maggie. She might be home. I proceeded to dial the phone direct from my house to Robinson Road in Bray, County Wicklow.

"Hello, hello."

"Hi there, Maggie. How are you? It's Pauline."

"Well, isn't this a pleasant surprise. How are you, and all the care?" She asked.

"We're all fine. The kids are getting big fast. They keep me hopping. Brad's working away. Mom and Dad are well. How's the weather over there?" I asked.

"Ah, the weather's grand. It's good to hear from you, fair play. Our family is well, and growing. You wouldn't know them. Charlie is still enjoyin' the sailing. I'm doing an evening class in accounting. We're all grand."

"Hey, Mag, how is Granny these days? I've been thinking about her."

"Mammy is here, Pauline. You can ask her yourself."

Granny wasn't so modern. She didn't have a telephone at her home. When her soft voice came across the Atlantic, my heart leapt. "Hello, hello. Who's there?"

"Hi ya, Granny. It's Pauline. I'm delighted I caught you in Bray. How are you keeping?"

"Oh, hello there, Pauline. Ah now, I'm not too well these past few weeks. Me ole legs are giving out on me. I've a devil of a sore on the one. Once a week a kind nurse comes in to give it a wash, and she dresses it. When a person reaches this stage of the game, they go to bed not sure if they'll see the sun shine, or be pushing up the daisies. But still, life is sweet at any age. So, and how's your Da? Tell him I was askin' for him. And your Ma, Colleen, and the boys?"

Granny sounded tired alright, but this was my Irish Granny, 'the swingingest Granny in town'. So I replied, "Oh Gran, you've got plenty of miles on you yet. You're like my old horse. You'll go forever."

"Pauline Kiely, are you callin' me an old horse?"

"No, no, Granny. I didn't mean it to sound like that. It's just my horse, Lady, is thirty-two; and that's really old for a horse, but she still goes like a teenager."

"Well, here am I, eighty-two, eighty-three come September, and not feeling the bit of a teenager. Say hello to your Da, will ya, and tell him I was asking for him."

"I will do."

"And Pauline."

"Yes, Gran."

"Unless you've won the lotto, we better get off the line. Never forget where you come from, Pet. Thanks for ringing, Love."

I sighed, and the line clicked.

The warm sun felt so good after the deep freeze of a dark winter. I love the seasons, and winter days can be glorious, but by March I've had enough winter. I'm always anxious to hang up coats and swap heavy boots for shoes. April showers brought on

May flowers. I decided to go for a walk through the woods to *The Farm*. The valley would be covered with trilliums in bloom and there were wild lilacs and honeysuckles along the fence lines. I rounded the barn before I saw the grey concrete house. Local school bus drivers called *The Farm* hill, 'Killer Hill' because the grade was so steep. Dad said he preferred to be high and dry.

Dalkey spotted me; so there was no sneaking up on my Father planting seeds in his garden.

"Hi there, Paul. We're on the best side of summer."

"How are ya, Da? Ready for a cup of tea?" I asked.

"Sounds good, so does a ham sandwich," he said with that grin.

We sat comfortably under the umbrella of the patio set on the deck. I felt high from the warm sun and haze of green in the trees on the horizon. While the tea steeped, he ate his sandwiches.

I said, "I just had a chat with Ireland and I got to speak to Granny! I called Maggie's and she was there. She sounded tired until I called her an old horse. That got her Irish up."

"I bet. What else did she have to say?" he asked.

"She said she's not well. Her old legs are giving out. She said for me to tell you she was asking for you," I said.

There was a comfortable silence before Dad said, "Maybe I best keep an eye on the paper for a cheap flight."

"What's going in the garden this year?" I asked because I felt it was time to change the subject.

"Oh, the usual. Your Mother keeps naggin' me to make the garden smaller while I just plant the seeds that come in the package. I roto-tilled in a load of manure last fall, so I guess we'll see what happens. I've had enough of the garden for today. How about we blow the dust off those nags?"

Mom had gotten a part-time job at Cedarvale Retirement home, and Dad said he was practicing retirement. My husband was at work, and my children in school; so we saddled up and seized a couple of hours. My Da insisted Irish people should own horses. He said, "It's in the blood." He rode a semi-retired chestnut thoroughbred gelding named Rob Roy. Robby was a big, gentle horse with a white blaze between his kind brown eyes. An old injury to his right front knee made jumping out of the question, but otherwise he was sound.

My Mother said, "I am calling the glue factory to pick up that little bitch." Lady was that little bitch, and she was famous for jumping fences, and taking off. The years had not softened the old nag. I didn't ride her anymore, but if anyone dared it was still the same routine. If you let your guard down for a moment, she'd put the bit between her teeth, jerk the reins out of your hands, and bolt full steam back to the barn, stopping dead at the fence. Mom said her patience with Lady got up and went a long time ago, but she never phoned the glue factory.

Dalkey barked impatiently as I undid the latch on the barn door. He would jump on the door and bang it open. His tail whipped around in delight and anticipation. I was breaking in my new horse, Zorina, a fifteen hand Arabian. She had been primarily used for jumping on the Trillium circuit, so hacking on *The Farm* was all new. Zorina was a gorgeous animal, a pure white mare with class and charisma, that tossed her head. I never had to chase her, she came to me when I called her name.

I had all but forgotten this day and our conversation when in mid-August my Father announced, "I've just booked my flight to Ireland. I leave Tuesday, and I got a great deal at three-fifty return. I'm only going for a week – I'll surprise me Mammy."

That evening Brad was home. I was recapping the day's events, and mentioned, "Dad's going to Ireland Tuesday, popping over for a week, three-fifty return."

"That's a great price. What are you waiting for? Go see your Grandmother while you can. There's no point going to a funeral." Brad said.

I hadn't even thought about it. "Really?" I said, "Really, I'm off to Dublin for a week, in two days?" I lay in bed and my eyes were closed but my mind got no rest. I was over the moon and up with the sun. Mom and Dad were still sipping coffee when I bolted through their kitchen door. "Dad, get me a ticket. Brad says I better go and see her while I can!"

"Well, get in line" he said, "your sister just called and apparently Cameron said the same." It was naturally assumed that our Mother would take care of our children for the week, and that included Colleen's newest addition, fifteen month old Lea.

Dad was always giving out to Colleen, "Why in hell did you give that little red head a French name? She should have been a Shelagh or a Nelly." He called the child "Lea-rua." He said this was "Lea the red" in Gaelic.

John Kiely and Lea Marie Duffy - 1993

Our Mother, our anchor, could always be counted on. She came through with an endless supply of common sense answers, comic relief, and unconditional love. Mom was genuinely happy to see her daughters go on holiday, and was only too glad to spoil her "little munchkins!"

Memère said, "It's only a week."

After a jig in the kitchen we called the travel agent and booked the tickets. By the grace of God 'the three amigos' were on the plane heading for the *Old Country*. We'd considered calling ahead, but Dad insisted, "We'll be there soon enough."

Seating on the Air Canada jet was tight; so thank good-
ness, my Father, being large-framed, had an aisle seat. Colleen
and I sat together a few rows ahead and across the aisle. We
kept each other company while Dad chewed the ear off an elderly Irish farmer, a Mayo man. Every so often I'd turn around to
check on me old fella and had to laugh at a pair of middle-aged
women in the seat behind him. The woman seated directly behind my old man appeared to be measuring how far his shoulders stuck out past the seat with her hands. Her friend next to
her elbowed her, winked, and the two of them shared an inside
joke.

It went from night to day, and after seven hours in the
air, we were relieved when the pilot announced, "Ladies and
Gentlemen, we will be descending into Dublin now. Nine-thirty,
Irish-time. Please fasten your seat belts as we begin descent."

As we made our way through the airport, out to the buses, and into the Fair City, banners reading 'The Dublin Horse
Show, August 16th to 21st' caught my eye.

"Hey, what's the date today?" I asked.

"It's the fifteenth," Colleen answered.

"Well, feckin' hell, Ripley's Believe It or Not, we're here
for the Dublin Horse Show."

This was a big deal for the three of us who had long ago
decided heaven on earth was in the saddle. Colleen was beat,
and she dozed off on the bus before we got to the train station.
Once on the Dart we enjoyed the scenery and Irish accents, and
we landed in Dalkey station in no time. Blue sky and cumulus
clouds welcomed us as we were once again reunited with the
cobblestone seafront village. Dad's chest pumped out. He was
home, with his girls, to visit his Mammy. Granny lived at 2 St.
Patrick's Square these days, just around a corner and down the
steps from the Dart station. Lace curtains covered her window,
and we stood outside the door listening to familiar voices inside.
Kate, Maureen, Maggie, Jenny, Colm, and Ellen were visiting.
Colleen and I were snickering with our cases in hand. Dad
tapped *shave and a haircut* on the door with his big knuckles.

Then we heard Maureen say, "John Kiely, if that's you, you didn't surprise me."

We were surprised. How did she know? When the door flew open and she saw Colleen and me she closed it again and said, "You dirty buggers. You did, you got me."

When Granny opened the door, her black eyes were shining. She was wearing a pink summer dress and black islet running shoes. Granny was smiling as she moved backwards, almost falling into her faithful chair.

"Hooray, John is here to take me down the country." said she.

Maggie became emotional, and her ginger-haired young lad, Colm, said, "Now, look what you lot are after doin'. You've made me Mammy cry."

Little Ellen, the image of her mother, consoled Maggie. "Ah Ma, 'tis only your brother."

Jenny flitted about the place like a butterfly, "Would you believe it? A knock comes at the door, and 'tis Canada on the other side."

We hugged, and then, of course, enjoyed a sacred pot of tea. Maureen informed us that she'd been tipped by a niece, who was spending the summer in Canada.

"And it's a good thing too. Are you lot completely mad all together? Jesus, John, you're old enough to know better. It's a terrible fright you'd be giving Mammy, just knocking on the feckin' door like the shaggin' neighbour looking for a bit of sugar or a few biscuits."

Aunt Kate elbowed me and asked, "Where are you staying?"

I whispered back, "With you. Will you have me?" And we hugged again.

Then she extended the invite to Colleen. Dad said, "Right then, we're set. I'll stay here with Mammy and sleep on the settee; and you girls are up the road with your Aunt Kate."

After the tea we all walked down to Killiney beach, except Granny who'd decided to stay in for a rest. The smell of the salt

water, the waves rolling into shore, and there was Dalkey Island
set out in the bay. They insisted I had to go for a swim. "Come
on, Pauline. It'll do you the world of good." Dad said.

About waist high I was gasping, and I realized this water
wasn't getting any warmer. I asked, "Are you people dead from
the neck up or down? When did freezing become refreshing?"

"Come on," Maureen insisted, as her head bobbed past. I
took the plunge and was breathless. Gasping for air, I thought
to myself, "A numb body with blue lips that is losing feeling in
fingers and toes is refreshing to the Irish?" I couldn't believe it.
In hindsight that very act of catching the first deep breath after
not being able to breathe is invigorating.

After the swim the kids inhaled Mars Bars. They each
devoured two, one for each hollow leg! We sat together on the
pebble beach and snapped a couple of pictures. Things were not
very good at home with Brad and me. I drifted off in thought
about how just before we came away, two weeks ago last Friday,
Brad was late, and my parents were at our kitchen table. The
kids had just gone to bed, and I greeted my husband at the top of
the stairs with a peck of a kiss. Our eyes locked because he
smelled of fresh sex. I was heartbroken, disgusted, and speechless. Brad simply excused himself, "I need a shower."

"What is there to talk about?" He said, "If you really
knew me, you could never accuse me of the things you do."

"I may be new, but I'm not that new." was my reply.

My weight was up maybe twenty-five pounds from our
wedding day, and Brad had reminded me of this again during
the last argument that we had had. He was never home; and
when he was, we were like fire and ice. Sweets seemed to call to
me when I felt depressed. I appear to be pulling down my bathing suit cover-up in the photos.

Maureen casually mentioned once or twice, "The pubs are
on strike." After a day or two I noticed people in pubs, and said,
"The pubs are not on strike." And Auntie Maureen said, "I'm just
winding you up, Pauline. The pubs in Ireland have a hard time
staying closed for one day of the year, Christmas day."

The walk back to Granny's was so pleasant. We walked along a green boarded wall. Just ahead there was a door, and it was ajar. I opened it up and stuck my head in to take a look around at this estate and grand garden. Colleen and Colm came in behind me.

Colm said, "That's Bono's house from U2. Apparently it was ransacked by vandals a few days ago. It was in the papers." An elderly gentleman was coming towards us, waving a stick. "Whoosh, you lot, go, go on now. Back out the gate. Away with you now."

I laughed and said, "No wonder, would you get a load of security."

We didn't run, we just stood there, and when the old gent got closer, I said, "My sister and I are big fans here from Canada. Our Da is from Dalkey. Is Bono home?" He had a thick black belt, with a billy-stick, but no gun. His white hair stood on end in the breeze as he said, "If you were up to speed on your celebrities, you'd know they're in Australia. Now be on your way, and I'll be locking the gate behind you."

We were still giggling about standing on Bono's lawn when we arrived back at Granny's. There she sat rocking in her chair. Every few seconds she'd hiccup and put her hand to her mouth. Rocking and hiccupping and hand up and pardon me, rocking and hiccupping and hand up and, "Oh dear, pardon me. I'm after eatin' a pair of those frankfurthers!"

Colleen said, "What?"

And said she, "Frankfurthers."

"Frankfurthers - you mean hot dogs?" Colleen clarified, "Granny, do you know what we call hot dogs in Canada? Lips and arseholes."

Granny looked stunned. Then she blinked a couple of times, and did she start rocking and burping and laughing. The look on her face was priceless. Then she popped up with her cane and shuffled towards the kitchen. She picked up the kettle and held it in the air, "Who's for tea?" When she was up I noticed how thin she was, and how swollen and red her ankles and calves were. Her hair was coarse, just shades of grey now. Her cane had been plastered in stickers by Maggie's kids. She used to twirl it like Charlie Chaplin to entertain them. Granny told me of her first love, a silent film star. She'd said, "He was gorgeous, God bless him. You do know what killed Ruddy Valentino, don't you? He died young because he wasn't allowed to pass wind in public."

"Granny, we're here because you told me you were sick." I said.

"And so I was. A dreadful thing, that." and she used the stick to point at the bandaged leg. "You see that; the swelling is down. 'Twas twice that size. Only for the good nurse that comes in and soaks it, and dresses it; and the sergeant there, Kate, driving me in to Dublin that I'm here today at all. 'Tis only better a fortnight now," said she.

Dad said, "Well, then, I guess you've been shaping up to go down the country. Will I see to hiring a car? The Horse Show is on, Ma; so the girls and I will catch that tomorrow and then we'll go down to Navan and visit Joseph and Shannon. We're only here a week."

"A week; sure that's barely time for tea." said she.

Then Dad asked, "Who fancies some Donegal catch? I'll pop over to Super-Value."

Over coffee and breakfast Aunt Kate filled in Colleen and me. It was Ladies' Day at the Horse Show. "Women will be dressed in their finest gear, and it's a big day for hats."

Dad came calling. Colleen wore a cute little denim ruffled skirt and jacket. Her sheriff star broach which completed the outfit was a total foreigner give-away. I chose to wear a cotton print dress with a big lace collar. We were grown up, and ours was a healthy friendship.

We were through the gate and in the stands before I said, "Pinch me," and Colleen did, hard. The stands and grounds were so well done and maintained. First we took in the parade of stallions: some magnificent horse flesh, thoroughbreds from the Irish National Stud Farm. Then mares with this year's colts and fillies entered the ring, and the young ones danced and pranced. The crowd said, "Oooh and aah." Colleen nudged me and pointed, "That one's mine. I'll hide it in my suitcase."

Kerry Gold Butter was the major sponsor of the event, and festivities were under way with a hunt demo by the Galway Blazers. All the riders turned out sharp, wearing their "Pinks": red jackets, black boots, and caps. The Hunt horn sent the hounds to tracking, and horses and riders taking the odd jump. To me the ultimate ride would be cross-country to hounds, "Tally-ho", and all that tradition.

There was a musical interlude while the crews set up a larger, tighter jump course. We went tinkle, but ran back to our seats when we heard the trumpet blast signalling the main event was about to begin. It was the International Scurvy. Stadium jumping representatives were present from all over Europe. A brilliant display of equestrian athletes, many of whom would be competing in the Olympics later in the season, representations from France, Italy, Belgium, the Netherlands, England, Germany, and Ireland, of course.

The grand finale was a brick wall competition. Each country selected one team representative to jump what appeared to be a six-foot red brick wall. This faux brick wall rose quickly to challenge the last teams competing. One rider lost his temper with his horse when he was disqualified, and he repeatedly hit the horse with his crop. That rider was booed.

We were on the edge of our seats when the wall rose to be over eight feet; and left in the arena were France, England, and Ireland. A young lad sitting behind us could faintly be overheard, "Da, Da! What do we do if the English win?"

His father countered, "Don't be worryin' yerself just yet, lad. Ireland taint trew."

France approached, and clipped the block. "Aaaahhhhh," sighed the spectators. The French rider tipped his hat to the audience, and was sent off to a big round of applause. Next came the British rider, and once again the stadium hushed to hear hooves pound the earth and up, up, over. He cleared, wow! Applause. Now it was up to Ireland, a small man on board a great grey. The announcer said, "This horse is an Irish Draught." The jump was so high they were out of sight, and then they appeared and . . . and, over clear, hip hip hooray, and the big grey kicked up his heels. When he did, he let go a blast of a fart that echoed through the stadium. The crowd was on its feet, and my old man had tears streaming down his face when he said, "Did you see that? Would you believe it?"

His big hands were still clapping when it happened the way it was meant to. The heavens opened up, and down came one of those famous Irish downpours. I guess the angels decided to show their applause by having a wee. The course was soaked in minutes. England and Ireland had tied for first.

Nothing had to be said. 'The three amigos' dashed out of the stands and hurried down to the stables to congratulate this rider. More importantly, we wanted to get a closer look at his famous farting horse. Afterwards we took a walk through the market and looked at fine saddles and other riding gear. When we noticed the "horses for hire" pamphlets, the thought crossed our minds, "Hey, maybe, we can go riding while we're here?" We were high and chatted about the day and the possibility of riding in Ireland all the way back to Granny's. Dad said, "It's a bit pricey to hire a car and horses for an afternoon; so it will be either a trip down the country or riding! We'll have to play it by ear."

When we got back to Granny's she had her television on loud, and until Colleen turned it down we were all shouting. We were recapping the events of the day, and said she, "You lot are completely mad altogether. Do you hear yourselves? And here I've been all day t'inkin, t'inkin about how good of you it is to come, and how happy I am that you girls and my John are here to see me and all."

As we ate our evening meal, the horseshow highlights came on her tele. Colleen turned it up a little, and pointed at a chestnut on the screen and said, "Hey, Granny, there's a horse like Dad's Robby back home."

"Your Father on a horse. You must be joking. Surely a man the size of your Da could give the horse a carry. Tis' an elephant he should be riding."

"I'm not that fat, Mammy. Here's the big grey. Now watch this." The three of us were hypnotized as we watched this magnificent animal give it his all, and that celebratory big buck finally, but what we heard and what really happened was drowned out by applause.

Dad said, "Ma, the girls and I were talking about maybe hiring some horses while we're here, but if we do we won't be able to afford to go down the country? Are you up for a couple of days down the country if I get a car?"

Granny responded firmly, "Be jaysus, just whom did you people come to this country to visit, me or the flippin' horses? Horses! Horses! Horses! The lot of you are horse mad!"

"So I'll be hiring the car in the morning. We'll take a drive out to Meath."

Chapter Seventeen

No Poverty
between the Sheets

T he morning was grey when my Father told his Mother,
"Mammy, the girls and I are off to get the car." Her reply
was unexpected. "You lot go on without me. I'll not be
able to join you this trip. I'm after not sleeping well. Me old
stomach is acting up, I'll be alright, so, go on." Granny certainly
wasn't herself this morning.

When we walked outside, the mist was so fine that it was
as if we were walking through clouds. The trip into DunLaoghaire on the Number 8 was relatively quiet. Colleen and I waited in
a black Honda while Dad filled out the paperwork required to
hire this car for a few days. Rain poured down the windshield
and the windows became steamed up, so we couldn't see out of
them but we didn't care because we were in Ireland! Finally he
emerged from the building and ran to the car, getting into the
right hand driver's seat. "Alright, girls, all set?" he said as he
fastened his seat belt.

Colleen said, "Ya, we're set, but we were talkin' and we
want Granny to come, Da. This doesn't feel right. We did come to
see her, and now we're taking off on her."

"Don't worry. I bet the ole girl's waiting for us. We have to swing by the house anyway because I forgot my camera. We'll see what she's up to now . . . I have a feeling she may have just needed a bit of privacy for a movement."

It was a hang-on-to-your-hat-if-you-had-one ride, riding in this little car weaving and bobbing through the narrow winding streets. As a passenger who is used to driving, the round-a-bouts were especially invigorating. Our car came to a halt. Dad set the hand brake. Granny opened her hunter green front door. There she stood in her tan London Fog coat, stick in one hand, and her bag in the other, "It's about time you lot got back here. I'm ready to go, gone twenty minutes now. Me overnight bag is just inside here, John."

Colleen and I said nothing, but were delighted. I moved into a backseat so Granny could be his co-pilot. She was in her element and leaned on the shoulder of her son as we made our way through Dublin traffic. I had to hand it to him, shifting gears on the opposite side of the road through the busy city with his mother leaning on him, saying, "John, is that O'Connell Street?"

"Yes, Mammy."

"John, is that Stephen's Green?"

"Yes, Ma."

"John, do you know where we're going?"

"Not really, Mammy. Maybe you'd better drive."

She sat up straight and smiled, and we passed the gates and grounds of Phoenix Park. "I should like to spend a full day there sometime", I thought.

A series of turns and jogs, stops, lights, and roads delivered us out into the quaint country villages where traffic was lighter and our driver could relax. Granny was smugly rubbing the right pocket on her cardigan when she announced, "I've sixty quid in here that says I'll stick the bill for lunch at the Ardboyne."

Dad said, "The Ardboyne? Jaysus, Mammy, these girls can't afford the Ardboyne, and you'll need twice that for lunch there." The Ardboyne was a high end, first-class hotel that held a fond memory in the old girl's heart because a couple of years back herself, my Mother, Father, Maureen and Harry had spent a night there.

Granny said, "The price, not a bother. Sure, me days are numbered. How will it be if I just write a dud cheque?"

Lunch time had long passed, so we ended up stopping at a pub somewhere for a bite to eat. It was a nice place, and we were seated in a solarium nearer the back. We looked over our menus, and made ourselves comfortable. A young lady came over, "Hello, are you ready to order?" she asked. We were, and ordered sandwiches and pots of tea. The food hit the spot and as we were washing it down, I smiled at the memory of a story aunt Brenna's friend, Amy Raferty, had shared with me when she was visiting last summer. Amy said, "I bumped into your Granny and we went for tea and sandwiches at Bewdley's in Dun Laoghaire. The server came to the table and asked, "Would youse care for anything else?" Yer Granny said, "Have you a tap in the kitchen, you know, running water?"

The young one said, "Yes, Mam, yes, we do."

With that she popped out her teeth and said, "Would you be so kind and give these a rinse for me then?"

Amy said, "There was an awkward silence until I spoke up and said, 'Could you just bring us a glass of water?' and there we were drinking the dregs of the tea with her false teeth in a glass on the table."

When Granny noticed some young people looking at us, said she, "You needn't mind them. Their day will come. Sure 'tis only a ha'penny looking down on the shilling."

With full bellies we ventured on. The weather had lifted and we were enjoying the sights and scenery. Most of Granny's sights were seen from her front seat as she wasn't about to climb in and out of the car or up the steps or hills.

When we stopped yet again, said she, "Old ruins, old ruins. For the life of me I don't understand why you people wish to spend your days with these old ruins?"

Colleen Duffy, Granny Kiely, John Kiely - 1993

So I said, "That is a mystery, considering we have one in the car? Ah well, we're here so we may as well check it out."

"John, do you hear this rip referring to her Granny as an old ruin?" said she.

"Don't mind her, Ma!"

It was lashing rain again as we neared the town of Navan in county Meath. Our little car shook with fear when big lorries passed. Dad asked, "Mammy, which is the road to Joseph's? I'd like to bring the girls by to meet him and Shannon."

"I'm not sure of the road to Joe's, John, but there's the road to the Ardboyne," said she.

"I've told you, Mammy. The girls can't afford the Ardboyne, and I'd like to introduce them to cousin Joseph; so please tell us, where's the road?"

"John, could we not just have a cup of tea at the Ardboyne?"

"Mammy, we will have tea with Joe and Shannon!"

The wipers were working furiously to clear the windshield. Big lorries whooshed past. We were passing the road to the Ardboyne again. Her directions had taken us in a circle. His face was red and his voice raised. "Mammy, for Christ's sake, tell me the road to Joe's!"

"I want to go to the Ardboyne," she challenged, and crossed her arms over her chest.

He pulled the car over and facing her, he spit a bit as he roared, "For the last time, the road to Joe's!"

"Well . . . isn't this a holiday to hell. Go on then, down the road and I'll show you the way." When we arrived at Joe and Shannon's, it was apparent they were out.

At dusk, about nine-thirty, we neared the village of Kells. The weather had cleared again when our Honda stopped outside an inn, The Kells Inn. "Why are we stopping?" Granny asked.

"I thought we might spend the night, Ma." Dad said.

"Ah, John, here, this place is a kip. Take me back to Ash town," said she.

I pulled a touring book out from a pocket behind her seat, and was quick with a makey-up.

"Granny, it says here that this Kells Inn serves the finest breakfast in all of county Meath. There's coffee or tea, fresh eggs, rashers, bacon, sausages, black and white pudding, scones, or brown bread."

She loved her grub. "Right, then. Will we go in for a cup of tea."

The warm Tudor Inn was lovely. There was a large chandelier in the dimly lit dining room visible from the front desk. Once we were checked in, Granny muttered, "Tis certainly no Ardboyne, but I suppose it will have to do." When Dad went out for our bags he realized he'd locked the keys in the car. We almost panicked until he said, "We are in Ireland. How hard can it be to find someone who can break into a car? You girls go on up to the rooms. I'll see what I can do?" It was a slow climb up moaning steps behind Granny and her cane to the second storey. I passed her in the hallway, went ahead, and opened the door to their room. Granny shuffled down the hallway like a penguin. I had just closed the door behind us when she stopped in her tracks, and announced, "I'm sick, sick over your Father lockin' them keys in the car. If I give you pair these, will you pray on them?" And from the left and right pockets of her overcoat she pulled out rosary beads for everyone. Colleen said, "Sure, Granny, we'll say a prayer." With that, a knock at the door and it was Dad, cases in hand. "Problem solved," he said.

Dad and Granny shared a room and Colleen and I another a bit farther down the wainscoted hallway. Arrangements were made to get up early to see the sights. We'd let Granny sleep in, and be back about ten or eleven for breakfast. Colleen and I talked and giggled like the couple of kids we were. We thought about and talked about our husbands and children before drifting off. I slept remarkably well, nestled under down-filled comforters between crisp linen sheets.

We awoke to magpies' caws and little birdies' tweets and chirps on a clear sunny morning. With our tourist handbook and cameras in hand, Colleen, Da, and I set out to take in some sights. We found ourselves in an ancient place named the People's Park. The Tower of Lloyd is located there with graves dating back as far as 200 B.C. These were graves of sacrifice victims in pagan times. We discovered an altar set in the corner of a stone wall where Mass was apparently said during a time when it was forbidden. We went to a lovely old stone church, St. Columba's, where the cobblestone walkways led us through established gardens. At the back of this massive church stood a cobblestone round tower. From the ground there was no way in. The only access was a narrow door probably seven feet up; so I gave Colleen a leg-up, and scaling the stone, she climbed in. As she went up the tower around the stone steps, I read aloud from the tourist guide. "Hey, Coll, the door is like that so the enemies couldn't get in, and the slit windows give light and provide space to shoot arrows from." She was near the top of the turret when my sister shouted down, "You should see the view from up here. It's awesome."

"Colleen," I said, "according to this book some woman murdered her son in that tower in 1076."

"Aaaaahhhhh!!!" she screamed, "It's haunted." and she twirled down the steps and leapt out onto the grass. She was brushing herself off when she said, "Yuck, Jesus, that's gross."

A stone's throw from the church was a strange cobble-stone hut known as Columcille's House. Entering the door on ground level, we were greeted by a twenty-foot ladder. Once at the top of the ladder we entered the chamber of the monks who, while living here, had written a major portion of the legendary *Book of Kells*. In this small space, they worked diligently by candlelight, using inks made from local fruits and berries, on six hundred and eighty pages of calf skin. This most famous ornamental version of the Gospels in Latin was produced between four hundred and seven hundred A.D. The original volume remains intact at the library of Trinity College in Dublin, and each day a page is turned. We were completely lost in time until Dad glanced at his watch. "Shite, would you look at that. It's after ten. We'd better be getting back."

We walked briskly back to the Inn and I was a bit winded climbing the stairs when I crossed paths with the manageress on her way down. I smiled and huffed, "Good morning."

She asked, "Is that your Gran then?"

"Yes."

"That one certainly isn't lost for words."

When we entered their room we found Granny ready and waiting in a chair. Excited, we all started talking at once, but she held up her hand to announce, "I'm just after straightening that young one out, about me in here with your Da, and you two girls sleeping down the hall. I let her know that John is my son, and you pair are me granddaughters; so we won't be needin' any condoms in room 212."

Colleen and I burst out laughing. Poor Dad turned so red that he only shook his head and sighed, "Jaysus, Mammy."

Colleen & Dad at Tara Hill - County Meath, Ireland - 1993

The day remained clear, and everyone very much enjoyed driving along the country roads. We saw Slaine Castle, and the ruins at the Hill of Tara where legend has it St. Patrick himself lit the Pascal fire before the pagan kings. This act brought attention to Patrick, and got him arrested. This is when Ireland's most famous Saint proceeded to teach Christianity to the people, using a shamrock as a symbol of the Blessed Trinity, the divine mystery of the Father, Son, and Holy Spirit, three in one. We all climbed the turret tower of an old Abbey and watched black and white dairy cattle graze on the shamrocks below us.

Arriving back in Dun Laoghaire after six, sure enough Granny inquired, "Anybody fancy something to eat? I've still got me sixty quid. How about I treat at the Miami?" the Miami being her local haunt.

"The Miami it is." Dad said.

Once we were seated, a young lady arrived at the table with menus. Winking at Granny, she said, "You've brought some friends wit cha today?"

Introductions were exchanged. Colleen and I asked for fish and chips, please, and Dad ordered a half-chicken dinner. Granny, studying the menu like it was her first time seeing it, says, "I suppose I'd need a hack saw for the steak?"

"No, Missus, 'tis very good." the waitress said.

Then Granny asked, "Have you a leg of lamb, or a mutton chop?"

Patiently smiling, "No, Missus, there's no lamb on the menu."

Granny decided, "Right then, I'll have the other half of his chicken, with chips, a pot of tea, and four slices of bread with butter to start."

The conversation was light as our bellies grew full, and we joked, "That was a good snack. Now what's for dinner?" When our plates were cleared, Granny got that gleam in her eye. "Who's for afters?" said she, "apple tart, banana split, or how about a knickerbocker glory?"

"What's a knickerbocker glory?" I asked.

And Granny signalled to the waitress, with a twirling index finger and said she, "A round of knickerbocker glories."

When the monumental desserts arrived, we were hard pressed to believe our eyes. Layers upon layers of fruit cocktail, ice cream, whipped cream, chocolate sauce, served in tall parfait glasses crowned by a maraschino cherry. "Wow, this is a Knickerbocker Glory?" I clarified before indulging in an act of pure gluttony. About half way through I began to slow down and whispered to Colleen, "I bet you a pound Granny can't finish," and she uttered, "You're on." I have a healthy appetite, but for the life of me couldn't take another bite; while there sat my Grandmother, a slight woman, holding the parfait glass to her mouth and slurping up every last morsel. I lost a pound in money to Colleen but for certain gained a few after that meal. When the waitress delivered our bill, Granny insisted, "I'll have that." She elbowed my Father and said, "Tis a far cry from the Ardboyne, but a meal's a meal; and the Lord be praised, me belly's raised an inch above the table." Granny was studying the figures and calculations when the waitress, in passing, asked, "Is everything alright?" And she said, "The service was grand. I've a bit of a tough time payin' for a chicken that died of starvation."

Back at home Granny seemed very contented, chuffed with herself, rocking in her favourite chair. She shared stories of the days when she was a girl, and stories of the days when my Dad was a lad. Said she, "Back in the days when Jack and I were young and so in love, his father would give us a loan of his pony and trap on a Sunday, and we'd go for a picnic or down the country. Then the babies started to come, and they kept coming. He was a good man, my Jack. He came to me in a dream one night, asking for my forgiveness. Of course I forgave him. Which of us is without sin; we are all only flesh and bones."

Colleen asked, "Granny, if you were so poor, why did you have ten kids?"

"To be certain, there was no poverty between the sheets!"

*Granny Kiely and her clatter of children, Harry Darcey and Morgan
Mooney – 1958*

We laughed with Granny who commanded, "John, give us
a song!" and the festivities continued. Colleen and I joined in
when we knew the verses to *Old Maid in the Garret,* or *Seven
Old Ladies Stuck in the Lavatory, Paddy McGinty's Goat,* and
some of the traditional ballads like *Spencil Hill,* or *Danny Boy.*
Dad was always singing these songs. He'd admit he was no Pa-
varotti, but it wasn't about being the best in the world; it was
about being a good sport and having a bit of fun. Granny finished the evening off with a poem:

> *"Mrs. McGraw is in need of a bra,*
> *while Mrs. Kelly needs a wash cause she's smelly.*
> *Poor Mrs. Keith has lost all her teeth,*
> *and it's Mrs. McNair who has the wild hair.*
> *Mrs. McGee needs to go for a wee,*

and there's Mrs. McGuire
who scratches her itch with a wire.

Our seven days went by too quickly. I didn't want to leave and just couldn't bring myself to say goodbye. Embracing my Granny, I confided, "Granny, we came here to charge your batteries, but you've charged ours. I won't say goodbye. How about, until we meet again. I love you, Gran."

And says she to me, "Pauline, you're a great girl, like a ray of sunshine coming into a room. Until we meet again. Best regards to Brad, and the young ones."

This was to be the last time I saw my Grandmother, Elizabeth Kiely, nee Johnston. During her lifetime the world had survived many technological and social changes, and she did her best to keep an open mind and never lose sight of her faith in God or humanity.

Indeed she had been sick, but not once did I hear her complain. By the following spring, the disease had spread completely through her body. After an attempted surgery the doctors said, "That woman is so full of cancer we don't understand why she is still with us." When Granny awoke from the anaesthetic, surrounded by all her children, said she, "I must be on me way out. Why else would you all be here? You know, I considered passing, but with the price of a funeral these days I decided to stick about."

When being transferred to the hospice by ambulance, Maggie was at her side. "Mammy, are you alright? Do you know who I am? Do you know where you're going?"

Ever so weak, said she, "Child, do you think I've lost the bit God gave me? Of course I know who you are, where I am, and where I'm going."

My Mother and Father went back to the *Old Country* twice since 'the three amigos' had our adventure. I wrote letters to Granny and Aunt Kate every chance I got. On May 23, 1994, my telephone rang, and my Mother said, "Pauline, I've had some bad news. Your Grandmother passed away this morning. Kate just called."

I consoled myself, "Well, she was eighty-four, and she did live a full life. At least she isn't suffering anymore." I absently returned to what I had been doing; and not really thinking I muttered, "Goodbye, Granny," Then something pierced my heart and I hit the floor in a heap. I sobbed, knowing this world, and our family, had suffered a great, great loss. My Granny whispered to me in a dream, "Cancer is a terrible way to die, and knotted up in secrets is a terrible way to live."

The demands of a young family left me strapped to a tight budget and unable to attend my Grandmother's funeral. My Mother and Father returned from this trip not wanting to talk about it. But he did say, "The church was packed. All her relations came from the country. Even some of the girls from the Post Office were there." He handed me a memorial card with his beloved Mother's picture on it that read:

Death is nothing at all. I have only slipped away, into the next room.
Whatever we were to each other that we are still.
Call me by my old familiar name.
Speak to me in the easy way which you always used.
Laugh as we always laughed at the little jokes we enjoyed together.
Play, smile, think of me, pray for me.
Let my name be the household word that it always was.
Let it be spoken without effort.
Life means all that it was; there is absolutely unbroken continuity.
Why should I be out of your mind because I am out of your sight?
I am but waiting for you, an interval, somewhere very near, just around the corner.
All is well. Nothing is past; nothing is lost.
One brief moment and all will be as it was before,
Only better, infinitely happier, and forever.
We will all be one together in Christ.

Chapter Eighteen

Four Seasons

Heading east on Highway 401 on our way to a Winter Carnival in Gatineau, Quebec, the passing transport trucks sprayed our sled-dog truck with a shower of water and road salt. It was February, and the snow in our headlights turned to slush upon impact with the ground. We had coaxed my Mother to tag along as she was to be our translator.

My Mom had become Memère. Everyone called her Memère. She said I caused her hair to go grey, but she kept it medium brown thanks to Lady Clairol. She didn't roll her own smokes, but she did think tobacco was a cure-all. When my old man nagged, "Cigarettes are bad for you." She'd reply, "You just want one." He'd say, "Lovey, the trouble with the ciggies is we don't just have one . . . it's one after another after another. The tobacco companies love it, they're so addictive; so in no time you're onto a pack a day. Then you live your life hooked on their product burning your money."

We were mushers in our dog truck, racing Siberian Huskies and Alaskan Huskies which are predominantly Greyhound and Husky crosses. It was quite a rig, the crew cab of our vehicle was comfortable, we were warm and dry, and the kids and my Mother practised their French by singing Alouette:

> **Alouette, gentille Alouette**
> Lark, nice lark
> **Alouette, je te plumerai**
> Lark, I will pluck you
> **Je te plumerai *la tête***
> I will pluck *your head*
> **(Je te plumerai *la tête*)**
> (I will pluck *your head*)
> **Et *la tête***
> And *your head*
> **(Et *la tête*)**
> (And *your head*)
> **Alouette**
> Lark
> **(Alouette)**
> (Lark)
> **O-o-o-oh**
> Alouette, gentille Alouette
> Alouette, je te plumerai
> **Je te plumerai *le bec***
> I will pluck *your beak*
> **(Je te plumerai le bec)**
> Et *le bec*
> **(Et *le bec*)**
> Et *la tête*
> **(Et *la tête*)**
> Alouette
> **(Alouette)**
> O-o-o-oh

I wondered how many miles we put on ourselves in a life-time? As Brad liked to drive, he said he was a road warrior hauling dogs, kids, and clan to dog races, munching M & M's to stay awake through the night.

Lacey was twelve, LeeAnn had just turned eleven, and Dylan was eight years old. They kept me busy, but it was actually a lovely time in my life. I turned so I was speaking to my Mother, "We were watching television the other day and this Always commercial comes on. You know, with or without wings, sanitary napkins. So I said to the girls, 'We're going to have to talk about that because soon you'll be getting *'your friend'*. And LeeAnn says, "You better talk quick Mom 'cause we both have pubic hair."

It was crisp and cold when we arrived at the race site, about 8 a.m. The temperature was minus 14 Celsius with plenty of snow. We zipped up and bundled up, and then filed out the doors on either side of the vehicle. The Gatineau Winter Carnival hosted many events between a lodge, party tents, and frozen shoreline. There was skating, hockey games, clowns, vendors, a snowmobile poker-run, and sled dog races.

Dylan at the dogsled races - 1996

Breakfast was stellar: delicious pancakes, waffles, crepes with local Maple Syrup, sausages, bacon, and flakey croissants. There were at least a thousand people or so there, so of course there was a beer tent.

At the race site our children had friends and snow banks, and we had fellow mushers to chat with before and after races. During race time we needed all hands on deck to drop dogs, harness dogs, and lead the team to the starting chute. Dog teams were started one or two minutes apart, and race results were calculated on a two-day time. Four dog class averaged four miles, and eight dog class, between eight and ten miles. There would be about twenty teams entered in both classes at any given race.

We could travel with sixteen dogs housed in eight crate-like compartments. Dropping dogs meant taking them out of the crates and snapping them to short chains welded to our customized rig. Then we could water and feed them, and the dogs could relieve themselves before a race. Training began in September with the dogs pulling an ATV. The racing circuit began in January, and there was a choice of races every weekend until early March. We were glued to the weather and followed the snow and race purses. The dogs were fed a high performance diet, and hydrated with baited chicken broth water.

Our 'North Force Kennel' was a strong and competitive team. This Frenchman was talking to my Mother about buying a dog. She switched back and forth from French to English as a light switch turns off and on. She sure came in handy, even if she was selling a lead dog that wasn't for sale.

The red-breasted robins had returned by the first of April when our phone rang unusually early. It was my Father and all he said was, "Is Lacey home?" His voice was stern. So I went upstairs, opened her bedroom door, and handed her the phone, still half asleep. I said, "It's Grandpa." Lacey's voice was very scratchy and when she said, "Hello."

"Lacey, your pony is loose over here, get your arse out of bed and put him in."

"Okay." She groaned and handed me back the phone. When I put the receiver to my ear he was gone.

Lacey got up, got dressed, and walked the twenty minutes to *The Farm*. When she got there her pony, Star, wasn't loose, but her Grandpa was smiling in the doorway, "April Fools! Come in here now and have some breakfast with me."

I had brought Dalkey a big bone with some meat still on it from a roast of beef we'd had a day or two before. There were still patches of snow and ice on the ground in late April. I knew he'd be mad at me because he couldn't come riding. As I couldn't go in the fields, I'd be riding along the side of the edge of roads.

It turned out he chewed through the bone before my unknowing Mother returned from grocery shopping. She opened the door on his pen because she was home now, and didn't understand why he bolted down the driveway. Big Red completely ignored her calls. When I came up over the crest of the hill on Zorina I saw our dog lying still on the road, with his bloody tongue hanging out. I galloped down the driveway and returned with my Mother and her car. By that time he had regained consciousness. We carried him on a blanket onto the back seat. I stayed home with the young ones, and Mom took Dalkey to a pet hospital in Fenelon Falls.

The Doctor on duty said, "His front left leg is broken in three places, and a section of it is shattered. They could amputate, or rebuild the leg with screws and a metal shank for twelve hundred dollars. My Mother called home. My Father said, "Who the hell wants to walk a three legged Irish Setter? Use your Visa. Fix the leg." My poor Mother felt so bad even though it wasn't her fault. They did the operation and kept him for observations overnight. When Dalkey came home my Father said, "Now, Shithead, if you don't come when I call you, I'm getting a big magnet."

The annual Beaulieu Family Reunion on the Civic long weekend in August is the highlight of the summer. The countdown begins when the school year ends in June. We are so blessed. Once a year all are welcome to gather on the sacred soil at Uncle Gill's, near Alban. Most years the sun is shining and you just can't beat it, 'cause you're in God's Country! The water is clean and cool, and we lounge around at the beach jibber-jabbering with well over a hundred family, friends, in-laws, and out-laws. Everywhere I look, people are engaged in conversation. Most of us have known each other all our lives. We're a blood line. My cousins Denis and Terry both have boats. They take my kids, and all the kids out skiing and tubing. There is a line to jump off the rock, and a couple of canoes for anyone to use. The Dionne's are pretty much the only other cottagers on this lake.

In the evening we change clothes, fire up the BBQ's, and as the sun goes down and the stars come out mosquitoes feast for an hour, but that's all. Then we sit around a roaring fire singing songs and telling tales. I look up to a blanket of stars and galaxies. I am not surprised only humbled if we are given the privilege of seeing some Northern Lights. The whole weekend is rough camping, clean air, and a steady hum of voices adorned with hearty laughter. I sat beside Jeannette who was sitting with Gail and Denise. She asked, "So how's it going, Paul?"

I replied, "It's going, Jeannette, just too fast. Look at our little girls over there, not so little, and suddenly we are our parents."

"Ya, I hear ya, remember when they were little and so sweet. They're like teeny-boppers now." Jeannette was referring to Marie, with Lacey and LeeAnn. My girls adored their cousin Marie. Every time someone had lost a tooth in our house, I'd laugh and say, "I must call Jeannette." Because when Marie was about eight she still believed in *The Tooth Fairy* and Jeannette overheard some kids laughing at her for this. So she took her daughter aside and said, "Marie, I'm gonna let you in on a little secret. I am The Tooth Fairy."

The next time Lacey and LeeAnn saw Marie she was wide eyed and bursting when she said, "Guys, have I got a secret. My mother is '*the*' Tooth Fairy, my mother, '*the*' Tooth Fairy. How lucky am I?" God bless her. It was classic. The mental image of my cousin with wings flitting around the world always made me smile.

My Mother's old Chevette that she gave to Jim ended up being a field car that my brothers bombed around *The Farm* in. Days grew shorter, and nights got cooler. The crops were off the fields, and like magic the maple trees turned yellow, red, and orange. One bright autumn afternoon my brothers showed up at my house wearing matching green work coats and they were calling each other Boris and Max. Jim was Boris and Sean was Max, and apparently they were Russian, and they said they were stupid but 'good-look-ink' and picking up chick-hens which is girls in dis country. Ya Vol.

Max said, "Hop in, baby. We take you for a spin!" I don't know what I was thinking, but suddenly I was introducing myself as Sasha, a 'super good-look-ink' who likes 'super good-look-ink' guys so will come for short spin.

I went inside to our mud room and shouted upstairs that I was just going for a car ride with Sean and Jim, and I took my hunter green London Fog off the hook to be Sasha joining Boris and Max.

Boris asks, "Max, where are we go-ink? What you tink-ing?

Max says, "Boris, we go up Politeski hill for their fair maiden, Christine. Maybe we kidnap-ink Queen's daughter, Boris. Dis is vot I is think-ink?"

I was in the back seat. Boris, wearing sunglasses, was driving on muddy trails with bald tires through hayfields. Max was not wearing sunglasses. Boris turned on the windshield wipers even though there was no windshield on this car, and he sprayed some windshield cleaner which got Max in the face. Max asked, "What kind of asshole is Boris? He is biggest asshole."

In early December The Bethany Hills Hunt Club hosted an annual Christmas Party that was geared for children and grandchildren. Ryan, Lea, and Dylan knew something was up about this Santa. He didn't have his glasses on and was buried under a white beard, but something was familiar. Was it or wasn't it? Lacey and

LeeAnn knew and were delighted as my Father hammered up the role of St. Nick. He had oats in his pockets for the reindeer. When he wasn't playing Santa, my Father led the room singing Christmas Carols. Accompanied by Sally Gibbs and her acoustic guitar, he encouraged us to sing at the top of our voices.

> *"Good King Wenceslas last looked out*
> *on the feast of Stephen.*
> *When the snow lay all about,*
> *deep and crisp and even.*
> *Brightly shone the moon that night,*
> *though the frost was cruel.*
> *As a poor boy came in sight,*
> *gathering winter fuel."*

To say my days were full is putting it lightly. Between the job, laundry, meals, and housework, horse chores, and dog chores, plus family obligations, the four seasons just went round and round. A heavy load. Some days I felt that if I were an elastic I'd have snapped. Other days I had the world by the tail and was walking on air. When I said, "Mom, you didn't tell me kids are twenty-four seven for twenty years."

She replied, "Someday you will see that your children become the jewels in your crown."

Chapter Nineteen

Tally Ho

When 'the three amigo's' returned from our holiday, I sourced out foxhunting. There was a serious club in York Region, and a not so serious club in Bethany near Peterborough. Being not so serious, I contacted the Bethany Hills Hunt Club, and Dad and I were invited out on an autumn Sunday afternoon hunt.

Robby was retired. My Father was riding his new black beauty thoroughbred named Molly; she had been a race horse, then a brood mare, and finally a riding horse. Her papers said Molly was fourteen. She had been used to hunt in Caledon Township a couple of seasons.

As much as the three of us had enjoyed galloping around at *The Farm*, Colleen could not persuade her horse onto the trailer. Young Bailey was still sort of green.

Dad and I were living our dream, riding with this hunt field. Our horses were groomed, well fed, and rested. We had our gear and tack all polished up. We were early birds to meet Kevin Harrison in Port Perry. In the background Da's homemade cassette tape of the tenor, Joseph Locke, sang, *Hear My Song.* We tailed Harrison's rig to the hunt host's location. I remember turning left on Dranoel road just east of Bethany.

It was October, and my watch had just gone nine o'clock when we were tacking up the horses. We were offered shots of port or sherry from silver trays, for courage. The contrasting fall colours were vibrant. The hunt field stuck to the edges of the worked fields, but in pastures we galloped. Zorina wore a red bow on her tail because she tended to kick; therefore I remained nearer the back of the pack. The view was alive with hounds tracking, tails wagging, horses snorting with anticipation. This was a good turn-out of twenty-odd horses and eighteen hounds. Senses and smells were heightened; and when the hound called "Hacksaw" suddenly bolted, the whip blew his horn and set off at a canter. "Tally ho!"

John Kiely on Molly at The Farm - 1994

It had been explained to us that the host had set the course, and gone around it dragging a burlap bag covered in animal scent. Basically this was a staged exercise for the hounds and the field. We were the field. A challenging four-hour ride for rider and mount. The jumps were less than ten, and no higher than three feet. You could always choose to go around. Everything was very casual, yet exhilarating. We had stumbled across some really great people who were horse-mad like us.

It was awesome being so focused, cantering Zorina in a pack. Through the bush I'd followed Ben Roberts on his big Belgian cross. I said his horse was like a bull dozer blazing the trail. Dad took his glasses off and punched me in the arm. Then he said, "We've found heaven."

He looked like he was ten years old and he didn't care when branches whipped us. Dirt was flung in our faces, but we embraced it because, if you understood, you knew it just didn't get any better than this.

The horses had a good lather of sweat on them towards the end of that ride. When I took the saddle off my white mare, all the dirt underneath had come to the surface leaving a steaming print. I walked Zorina until she naturally cooled down. Then we had lunch. A hearty stew, a sweet table, and brandies were offered by the club's past president, our hosts that first ride. The Master introduced himself, and invited us to join the field again. This was an honour that my Father and I were only too delighted to oblige.

Dad got right into hunting. He bought a bigger truck, and the three horse slant trailer. We rode on Sundays with our hunt friends that fall, the next spring, and fall.

Brad and I kept busy existing. There was never enough money. I had to work more hours. Dad and I had a disagreement; something about me having my own house and why was I always at *The Farm*. He was trying to run a business and have a meeting with Sean and Jim. I was so hurt and stressed out that I told him, "I can't play horsey with you anymore, Da." And in haste I sold Zorina to a riding school. Then Colleen sold Kella, and moved, Bailey, closer to her at a stable in Beaverton.

Mom continued to work part-time because her husband was home full-time. She said, "When he was thirty, I couldn't find him; and at fifty he asks me, 'What do you want to do today, Lovey?'"

One Sunday morning when the kids and I arrived at Mass the traditional two minutes late, they headed straight for the family pew. They knew the drill, as my whole life our family always sat twelve rows back, right side. The twerps were delighted to see his tweed jacket. "Grandpa."

His grey hair was combed to one side, and thick tinted glasses rested on the bridge of his nose. He called his trimmed moustache a cookie-duster. Lacey climbed over and snuggled up one side, LeeAnn squeezed up under the right arm, and Dylan climbed onto his lap.

I whispered, "What are you doing here?"

And he said, "Molly refused to get on the trailer!"

Then we blessed ourselves and did our Vatican aerobics - sit, stand, kneel, stand, sit. When the choir started up, my Father leans over and asks me, "Do you think they're getting any better?"

I was in a good mood, "Ya, sure, maybe."

It had been a long time since I really tuned into that out-of-tune organ and the creaky voices. I gave them an A for effort. And then my Father said, "You must be joking. That sound is like a feckin' nail going through my head every Sunday morning!" So my shoulders shook, and I had to bite my cheeks to stop the laughter for the remainder of the service.

Later that day our whole clan gathered in the dining room for dinner because it was Jim's birthday. He was the one who could computerize a shovel, the same one that our Mom called *the leader of the rectum gang* because he stole a couple of bottles of whiskey after Colleen's wedding, and hid it in the root cellar in the barn.

I can still remember how the sweet smell of the ham made us hold our noses a bit higher in hopes of taking in a little more, and my Mom removing the toothpicks on the pineapple rings now that it was cooked. The scalloped potatoes were done as well, but remained in the oven while the meat was sliced. Colleen carried the bread basket and butter into the dining room, and I brought to the table a garden salad with three choices of salad dressing - Kraft Italian, Catalina, or French. The electric knife hummed as it carved through the tender meat in the kitchen. The scallops came out of the oven. Some milk had bubbled over and left a black mark on the tin foil; but underneath, the self-cleaning oven was still clean. The hot food was delicious and very much appreciated after an afternoon outdoors. We were *The Walton's*, but we swore, smoked, and drank. So we weren't *The Walton's;* we were *The Kiely's*.

My Mother was in her element. She set the stage in her formal dining room, with ornate wallpaper above frames of white painted wainscoting. She camouflaged old windows with blinds, sheers, and drapes. We used the Waterford Crystal and the cutlery in the wooden box for special occasions. After a big feed, Jim blew out twenty-one candles.

Dad's spoon went ting tang but these days he was depressed about the economy. "Free trade and credit cards have ruined this country. Nobody can get ahead. I feel for your generation. I don't know what you lot are going to do when I'm dead and gone."

I said, "Here we go with the gloom and doom. Look around you. Really, do you want for anything? Why are you always moaning about the economy? Mom might die young from smoking, but you - you aren't going to die. You're gonna live forever, and be a garnish at the end of my table looking for a feckin' sandwich and a cup of tea."

When we were leaving, I was flying out the door to go around the block and put my kids to bed. I was down the walk only a few steps when my Father shouted, "Come back here, you little rip, and give your old man a hug."

He said, "I love you." And I hugged him back hard, and said, "I love you too."

Chapter Twenty

Superman

T he following Sunday on May 7th, 1995, at approximately 10:50 a.m., John Francis Kiely flew off Molly. They had rushed a jump, and collided with the rear end of a Hunt Master's big horse, named Sam. My Father was going too fast, and I should have been there to remind him to slow down, but I wasn't.

There is one rule in foxhunting; and that is, you don't pass the Master. Then there was his stand on that subject, "Rules are meant to be broken, or at the very least tested."

The last time I saw his mount, her dark coat shone. Molly was lonely, Dad was lonely, and the barn was lonely. His horse was in really high spirits, and it was as if she were trying to talk to us, whinnying and snorting. I remember now saying to him, "You shouldn't be feeding that horse all that high-test grain." He had read a book on horsemanship and been giving her generous portions of warm mash. I also remembered him saying more than once, "My Granddad would be proud of me! He would have loved this place." And I remembered about his Grandfather and Bubbles.

I can hear the horn, smell the earth in spring fields, feel the reins looped between my fingers, the heat under my saddle, and rhythmic breathing in beat with Zorina's strides. I wasn't there that morning. I wasn't there to remind you to 'cool your jets'. They said you cantered up to the rest stop; and as you came to a halt, just keeled over with that beaming smile that remained on your face until they closed the lid on the casket and lowered your body into the ground.

The Hunt Field was out in the wilderness of Cavan Township when the hounds caught scent. The majority of the group had gone on. The few remaining thought you passed out. Cathy and Ron, being veterinarians, stayed with you, and our dear friend Sally, of course.

The Hunt Master and his lovely wife were very distraught at your funeral. We were all still under the suspicion that you had had a heart attack. But we did discuss what happened, and from what I could understand, you were pretty shaken up and humble after the fall. The Master said, "Sam is slow, and Molly is fast. None of us could believe she was the same horse."

Sally Gibbs said she stopped and asked if you were alright. She said it was a bad fall alright, but you did appear to be fine, and that you were speaking as you brushed yourself off. She said, "When he popped back up on Molly, I figured he was alright. We rode on for another few minutes. I was ahead of him, and got to the rest stop first. John came cantering towards me, slowed his horse to a stop and just keeled over and hit the ground. "

An ambulance was called, but it was too late. Ironically they were treating you for a heart attack. Nine months later the autopsy report came back stating that your heart and organs were fine, that the impact of the fall had caused your lungs to fill with fluid; therefore, this death was the result of an accident.

We didn't heed your warnings. More than once you'd said as you were planting your trees, "I won't live to see these reach their maturity, but you will. You died too young, but you were doing something you loved, and with a big smile on your face. You lived life large. I consoled myself because at least you and Granny are together. My first thought was that when she arrived in heaven, Jesus may have said, "Lizzy, you're a Saint. All your life you gave. What can I give you in return?" and she may have just answered from her heart, "My John". Of course, it would be granted because he was hers first. We only borrowed him.

It was such a shock and so unexpected for all of us. This great giant family. Dad let us know that he hated women working as he respected their role in the home. It was even worse working on the day of rest. But I was on the job, my sister was at work, and my Mother was scrubbing away when he died. He gave us his opinion, "You girls should be at home with your families."

I had just topped up a tray of champagne flutes filled with Morning Glories for the Mother's Day lunch buffet at The Briar's Inn. The face on my supervisor showed no expression when she strolled over to me and said, "You have to go home, Pauline. Your husband just called. Apparently your Father has been hurt horseback riding."

I laughed, "Debbie, you should see my Da. He can carry a horse. I can't leave now; we're about to be slammed with the lunch rush."

"No, really, you'd better go," she said. "We'll manage fine."

As I drove passed the Sibbald's Point Park entrance, a voice inside me said, "People die falling off horses." A frigid chill ran through my blood and bones, and I pulled my Ford Taurus over to the beat-up phone booth at Park's Variety. I dropped in a quarter and dialled O. I wanted my Mom. When the operator answered, I said, "This is an emergency. I must get a hold of my Mother. She works at Cedarvale Retirement Home in Keswick." I was patched through. "Hello, this is an emergency. I must speak with Yolande Kiely. This is her daughter."

"I'm sorry, someone called earlier, and Mrs. Kiely has left for the day."

I hung up, jumped back in the car, and my tires spun dust.

My children were playing soccer on our front lawn as I drove towards our home on Old Shiloh Road. They appeared fine. They waved when they saw me, and ran towards the car. They hugged their mother, even in her dorky, polyester uniform.

"How come you're home so early?" my eight-year-old gappy-toothed son asked?

"I don't know. Where's your Dad?"

My big girl Lacey was twelve, and she said, "Dad's inside."

So I went inside, and ran upstairs, but Brad was in the shower.

"I'm here!" I shouted so he'd hear me.

Brad was scheduled for nightshift. I had just pulled off my stinky stockings, and was stepping out of the permanent press uniform when Brad entered the bedroom. He was still damp, and wrapped in a towel.

"Pauline, sit down."

"Why?"

"Just sit down, please."

So I did, on the edge of the bed, and he said, "It's your Dad. He didn't make it. He died this morning."

I looked at him with such disgust. How could he be so cruel? Why was he telling me this worst lie ever. Then it hit me that what he said was true, and a loud wailing sound came from deep inside me, and my body turned to mush. Brad attempted to put his arms around me to console me. Through tears, mascara, and snot, I asked him, "What? What happened?"

"The police were here, and they don't have all the details. They need a family member to identify his body at the hospital in Lindsay."

"Oh my God! My Mother! My poor Mother! Where is my Mother?"

"She's on her way. I've called her work," he said.

The kids came running up the stairs. "What's wrong? What's wrong with Grandpa?"

Lacey, LeeAnn, and Dylan saw the state of their mother; and so looked to their father for answers. "Grampa died today, guys. There's been an accident. Memère will be here soon. I've called Colleen's, and sent a message with a neighbour to the cottage for Jim."

I was dressed and downstairs when I caught a glimpse of her turning in to our drive way. As I reached for the door knob, Brad stopped my hand, and said, "Let her come inside."

I waited, but opened the door just as she grabbed for the knob. One look at the state of me told the story, and she screamed, "No! No! No! And she held me and hit me, and held me, and cried out, "He's dead? He's really dead?" I nodded yes, and she held me, and hit me, and wept, and hit me, and held me some more.

Colleen, Cameron, Ryan, and Lea showed up and we bumped into each other crying and hugging. The children imitated us. I felt like a stunned bird that had hit a window. I was there in body and hearing words and going through motions, but this just couldn't be real.

It was decided that the immediate family would all go to Ross Memorial Hospital, and Brad and Cam would stay with the twerps. The children adored their Grandpa. He had always taught them things and entertained them with his 'little ditties' like;

> *"There was a little fly that flew in the store,*
> *he shitttt across the ceiling, he shitttt across the floor,*
> *he shitttt across the bacon, and he shittt across the ham,*
> *and he shitttt all over the little grocery man.*
> *Singing na, na, na, na, na, na, na, na, na!"*

I'd said, "Dad, don't be teaching the kids that song, and he'd replied, "Why, it didn't do you any harm." I drove my Mother's car, with my sister and Mother as passengers, around the block to *The Farm*. Sean's Chevy van, the shaggin' wagon, was parked in the driveway. Dalkey circled Mom's car, and served as escort to the door. Mom, Colleen, and I came into the breezeway, and I coaxed the Big Red to come inside. As I knocked off my shoes in the breezeway, I could see my brother stirring his coffee. At twenty-four years old, Sean was a passionate carpenter, like his Father, and his Grandfather.

Mom said, "Sit down, Sean." So he did, but he was already on to us, "What's going on?"

"Your Dad passed away this morning, Son."

My brother's face went red, and his hands hit his eyes. "What are you saying, Mom? I felt something weird earlier, and I knew something was wrong."

Two of Jim's friends had recently lost parents. Fireman Joe Dowling had died from a massive heart attack and Mary Tremblay had lost her battle with breast cancer. When Jim heard the news he was shocked but not totally surprised. My little brother said, "I just knew it. I was driving home, thinking he must be dead. They wouldn't insist I have to come home if he were just hurt."

So we embraced, and sobbed, and the immediate family got into the car to identify the body in Lindsay Hospital. Sean drove the car that his Father drove on Sundays. My brothers sat up front with their Mother between them, and Colleen and I held hands and gawked out the windows in the back.

As Colleen also worked at a retirement home, I just assumed she would be better prepared for this. How could she be? This wasn't work. This was her Father, her family, her personal space. I thought how Auntie Theresa's voice had sounded when I called her before we left, so I assumed Ireland may know by now. Jim broke the silence, "Do you know what happened at work this week? Dad and I have been working on this gazebo deck and porch entrance at Carol Master's place. And Mrs. Masters bought this octagon window for the little porch entrance. She had been after him to put it in, but he kept procrastinating. He insisted it was a cheap window for a reason. He said it would leak. Anyway, on Friday she came out of the house and said, "John, I thought you would have had that window in by now?"

And he says, "You know what thought did? Pissed the bed and thought he was sweatin'."

Jim continued, "I had to jump off the deck and cover my mouth to stop laughing. The expression on her face, and the way she just backed into the doorway. It was classic!" We were racked in pain but managed to smile because that was our *Da*.

The nurses in Lindsay hospital didn't know what to do with so many bodies to identify one body. They put us in a room; and then they showed us what room he was in. We went in and paid our respects. There was something like a soother in his mouth, and his left cheek was bruised. He looked very peaceful. He was a big man wearing his Sunday best, even those Canadian riding boots that were so much better than mine from the U.S.A. His body was lifeless. It couldn't run, or sing, swing a hammer, or do anything without the energy of his spirit. This time last week we had walked in the orchard, and played 'No Laughing, No Talking, No Red Light!' and then we had made a family pyramid. How could you leave us? Where did you go? My heart ached. Every cell in my body pained.

On the way home Sean drove again. Our Mother, his wife, and the love of his life, broke the silence. "He was singing, 'What a Wonderful World' this morning as he was shaving. We could have lost him a couple of years ago when Dalkey went through the ice. And we should have lost him twenty years ago in that tractor accident."

And Sean agreed, "You're right about that."

Jim said, "No regrets. We were lucky." And Mom clung to that, but I felt so sick because I had not been there.

Brad had made some more phone calls. Uncle Dan and Aunt Brenna were at our house when we returned. Auntie Agnes, and Aunt Anne, and Bruce were on their way from Woodstock. My dear friend Ruth had lost her beloved mother to cancer, and she arrived with food, but I had no appetite. I reached for a bottle of whiskey. Uncle Dan said, "Sometimes that makes it worse."

"There's no way it can get worse." I said.

But it did because after a couple of shots I started screaming and pounding the kitchen counter and cupboards that my Father had built. "Who cares about this stuff when you lose someone you love." I was put to bed by my Mother. Our world would never be the same. She lay down with me, and we held each other and cried. I could hear my Daddy singing in my head:

"Oh, the sun it was setting in the west,
And the birds were singing on every tree.
Now when I'm far away on the briny ocean's tusk,
Will you ever heave a sigh or a wish for me?"

He passed away on a Sunday. To allow time for the family to fly in from overseas the funeral service was held at eleven o'clock the following Friday, the twelfth, a payday. Family, friends, neighbours, employees, employers - who wasn't there? People, in shock, had such kind sincere words, and we needed each and every one of those hugs. There were so many flowers, and so many visitors. Thank God for my Mom's sister, Anne, and her cooking, because she fed us for days. The day of his funeral a road crew working nearby asked Jacquie Marchand, "Who died, the Mayor?"

And she said, "No, it was my Uncle John."

My Father had touched so many hearts on his journey. He always said, "You take nothing but memories with you, and that's what you become." Mourners said, "Your Dad had great qualities: he taught me the trade, loaned me money, gave me a ride, gave me some good advice, believed in me when no one else did. He saved my life!"

Picking out the plot was a no-brainer because my Mother said, "It was the strangest thing. Around Easter your Father says to me, 'You can bury me in there when my time comes.'" He was indicating Briar Hill Cemetery in Sutton as they drove past.

She said, "The wave of relief I felt was amazing, him being Irish and all. I always wondered if he'd want to be buried here or over there. Little did I know his time would come within a month. Jesus, I finally get to buy a piece of real estate, and I can't even flip it for a profit."

The Church was packed, and we held his wake in a party tent in the back garden on *The Farm*. The day was hot and sunny, and noses and bald spots got scorched. There were blossoms on some trees, and the wild asparagus was up. We supplied a keg of beer, a few boxes of wine, plenty of coffee, and there was tons of food, thanks to the ladies from the choir and church parish. The Dubliners, The Clancy Brothers, Roger Miller, Chuck Berry, and Bill Hailey played softly in the background. There was a mixture of laughter and tears. Gary and Janice Keough took the day off and travelled three hours from Cambridge. I hadn't seen them in ten years. It was a big crowd for the wake, four hundred or so.

When I thought about it, I remembered my Father doing his good deeds and calling them "Brownie points for heaven." In the church, after I read his eulogy, Annette Straver got me to stop sobbing by pulling on my nose. She had a good idea how I felt because she had lost her dear mother in a tragic car crash only six months before. Laurie Wood, still our Eddie Haskell, said, "I don't know if I feel sorry for you. Your Dad rode horses, and sang all the time. He took you to Ireland, and built you a house." She was trying to help me see the bright side. I will be forever grateful to her husband, Rob Rogers, who proposed a toast, "To John Kiely, a man amongst men!" and everyone said, "Hip! Hip! Hooray!" three times.

In the days that followed, his horse paced back and forth at the fence, and his dog heaved and shed tears like the rest of us. It was unanimous; we chose a green granite headstone with a Claddagh symbol on it with the inscription, *"In my hands I hold your heart and crown it with my love."* I spent the better part of eight years lost before I found myself in The City of Kawartha Lakes and remembered where I came from.

When I arrived here, and opened the local phone book listed under Bethany at the top of the K page was the name, John Kiely. I couldn't believe this! So I phoned this John Kiely, and I left a message.

"My name is Pauline Kiely and I recently moved into Fenelon Falls. I was wondering if you were Irish? Perhaps you could give me a call?"

A few days later a heavy accent spoke on the other end of the line, "Hello dair, Pauline Kiely. 'Tis John Kiely speakin'. A Waterford man. A few year ago this horseman named Kiely was killed in these parts. Me neighbours were all callin' to see did I take up horseback riding? Any relation?"

"Yes, that was my Da. My great-grandfather was originally from Waterford, but my Da grew up in Dalkey. Would you be able to come out a week Sunday for a BBQ to meet the family?"

"Now wouldn't that be grand. Me spending me birthday surrounded by Kiely's. There's not many of us here you know?" he said.

"Excuse me, but just when is your birthday?" I asked.

Says he, "Me Da always said it was the thirteenth, but me Ma insisted it was the twelfth. So seeing as me Ma was in a better position and of clearer mind, I went with her date."

"Are you telling me June the twelfth is your birthday?" I said.

"Yes!" he answered.

"Well, that's my birthday; and that's why the family's coming out next Sunday."

"We'll look forward to meeting you then." says he, "Small world, but you wouldn't want to paint it."

Through it all we counted on our Mother. She taught us all to count our blessings, to see what we have. It was said more than once that my parents complemented one another.

Three weeks after my Da's accident, another Superman, actor Christopher Reeve, crashed off his horse. He survived, barely, because machines kept his body functioning. We all agreed our "man of steel" wouldn't have wanted that.

Alo told Oxo that Sadie was his birthday present because she was thinking of him when she had her daughter on his birthday. Dad always called Sadie, "Shelley!" Because a birth always follows a death, in August of '95, little Sadie Darcy, delivered triplets, two boys and a girl.

In December when my Mother's birthday rolled around she said, "My Mother died on May 5th, and both my Father and Husband on May 7th. I'm not the first widow, and I sure won't be the last. If I were my Mother, I'd be delivering a baby today."

The Farm that I wanted to put my Father in a straight jacket in a rubber room for buying, turned out to be the best years of our lives. On these 147 acres, with ninety workable, I celebrated the seasons with nature. We tapped tall maples in the spring for sap. I got stuck in the mud once or twice with a kid on my back. I always did my share of chores at the barn, and took advantage of the horseback riding.

My family and I watched a mother fox with her kits, and saw lots of deer, the northern lights, shooting stars, and even a rainbow or two over *The Farm*. When in flower, the hayfields would be bursting with butterflies. All seasons, my children and I hiked through pastures, cedars, and hayfields. We also had an alternate route via hardwood forest and the artesian well. It was longer, but definitely more picturesque. There would be animal tracks in the snow: bird prints, deer tracks, squirrel, rabbit, and mice trails. One time I came across a clear print of a large hawk or owl's wingspan. It appeared to have put an end to a mouse's journey. In winter pure white snow clings to everything: cedar rails smothered in grapevines, green trees, grey trees, white trees. Old trees can silence the wind. The snow is deeper in the forest. I remember pausing to catch my breath, and thinking to myself, 'Am I ever lucky, living in Mother Nature's living room.' I thought this would be forever, but I remembered what he'd said,

"Death comes to us all like a thief in the night. We know not the day, nor the hour. We're all links in the chain of life, and this I believe is life everlasting."

The prayer of Saint Francis of Assisi was on the back of my Father's memorial cards.

Lord, make me an instrument of Your peace.
Where there is hatred, let me sow love.
Where there is injury, pardon,
Where there is doubt, faith,
Where there is despair, hope,
Where there is darkness, light,
and where there is sadness, joy.
O Master grant that I may not so much seek
to be consoled, as to console;
To be understood, as to understand;
To be loved, as to love;
For it is in giving that we receive;
It is in pardoning that we are pardoned;
And it is in dying that we are born to eternal life.

*LeeAnn, Jim, Lacey, baby Lea, and Colleen
picking apples at The Farm*

THE CURSE OF IMMIGRATION

I was doing just fine in this life of mine,
                     my heart neatly tucked away,
when one summer's day, I found my way
                     to the shore of Dublin Bay.
I came for a rest, and enjoyed the jest
                     an outsider looking in.
Distant family kindly greeted me;
                     they tucked me under their wing.
Then the strangest thing it caught me quite by surprise-
My heart opened up, and I saw his hometown
                     through my Father's eyes.

Dear, dear old Dalkey, how you tugged on my heart.
Dad often wondered why he chose to part.

Canada is grand, a prosperous land,
                     but far from his native home.
With his fine wife, they've built a life,
                     four children to call their own.
"A foot" said she, "on each side of the sea
                     for an Irishman who did roam."
His old soul travelled back and forth, never knowing
                     which place to call home.

Dear, dear old Dalkey, how you tugged on my heart.
Dad often wondered why he chose to part.

Now he is gone, but his spirit lives on,
                     no more to be torn by the sea.
Rest in peace, good man, no more worry or toil,
                     for now your spirit is free.

While this is a true story, some of the names and identifying details of the persons, and places involved have been changed. Some events did not occur in the precise order or at the precise time related in the book. As with any writing, this story reflects only my perspective on events, and the book relates my perspectives. I do not mean to hurt or judge any others who are depicted in this story, especially because I am so grateful to all of them for their role in this journey. This book is intended to capture and portray the family traits of resilience and optimism.

Beaulieu Family Tree

Grandparents
Alice (Rancourt) & Eugene Beaulieu

Children
Lea, Gilbert, Bette, Oscar, Agnes, Paul, George, Dolores, John, Anne, Gabriel, Yolande

Lea & Ernest Marchand – Jacqueline, Alice, Celine, Yvette

Gilbert Beaulieu

Bette & Johnny Dionne – Yolande, Diane, Gerry, Reggie, Michelle

Oscar & Lise Beaulieu – Denise, Denis, Ginette *Denise & Marty Beatty – Keith

Agnes & Ross Tripp – Patsy, Gail, Gary *Patsy & John Hudson – Carrie, Candace
   *Gail & Eric Osso – Zac & Jeff

Paul & Jean Beaulieu – Darryl, Rae, Laura, Terry, Brenda, Rachel

George & Bernice Beaulieu – Chris, Jeannette, Marcel, Suzanne
   *Jeannette & Rick Timms– Marie, Derek, Wayne

Dolores & Gabe Villeneuve – Richelle, Richard, Rao, Lorraine

John & Frieda Beaulieu – Pat, Brian, Rick

Anne & Bruce Perry – Alan, Kim, Carolyn, Michael

Gabe & Olga Beaulieu

Yolande & John Kiely – Pauline, Colleen, Sean, Jim
   *Pauline & Brad Parsons – Lacey, LeeAnn, Dylan
   *Colleen & Cameron Duffy – Ryan, Lea

Kiely Family Tree

Grandparents:
Elizabeth (Johnston) & Jack Kiely

Children:
Pat, Theresa, Maureen, John, Kate, Dara, Moira, Peter (Padder), Brenna, Maggie

Pat & Gwen Kiely – Kerry, Michael, Tess, Orla
Theresa Kiely
Maureen & Harry Darcy – Thomas, Sadie (Shelley), Declan
John & Yolande Kiely – Pauline, Colleen, Sean, Jim
Dara Kiely
Kate & Dave Spang – Tina, Greg
Moira & Rory Gallagher - Stan, Will, Trixie
Peter (Padder) Kiely
Brenna & Dan Gildener – Jacob, Alicia
Maggie & Charlie Malloy - Jenny, Colm, Ellen

No Poverty Between the Sheets is the first book in a trilogy.

The sequel title, *Divorce is Dirty and Hell is Hot,* will be available in print and electronic versions in September, 2014.

For further information or updates visit:
www.paulinekiely.ca

Pauline Kiely has been an avid student of Creative Writing her entire adult life. This author has consistently taken various courses offered at University of Toronto, and Trent Universities. She has attended numerous readings, conferences, and workshops, and been an active member of the Writers' Community of Durham Region, Festival of Stories, and Pen House Magazine.

As a freelance journalist Kiely specializes in business profiles. Amongst her steady client base is the Economic Development Department of The City of Kawartha Lakes. To date she has been well received, and experienced success in national and international print and electronic markets.